MW00917301

Remaking
Manhood

Stories From The Front Lines of Change

Mark Greene

Remaking Manhood: Stories From the Front Lines of Change
Revised and expanded 2nd edition
Copyright © 2018 Mark C. Greene
All rights reserved.
Publisher: ThinkPlay Partners, New York, NY
ISBN: 1530817064

Dedicated to my father, Arthur Wellington Greene Jr., the man who taught me how to love unconditionally.

This book is also fondly dedicated in equal parts to my wife, Saliha Bava, and my son, Gus, without whom I would not be the very lucky man I am today.

Additionally, I'd like to thank the ManKind Project, a community of men who are striving for personal growth and connection. If you are a man who is suffering, reach out to them.

And finally, this book is dedicated to Lisa Hickey and the many remarkable men and women of The Good Men Project. They are changing the world for the better.

Contents

Introduction:
The Emotional Price of Manhood

For generations, America's culture of masculinity has taught boys and men to suppress their emotional expression. To this day, we coach our sons to present a facade of emotional toughness and our daughters to admire that facade in men. Even in infancy, little boys are expected to begin modeling emotional stoicism, confidence, physical toughness and independence. The strong and silent type remains a central American symbol of "real manhood."

When we instead choose to encourage the full range of human capacities in our children, growing strength and self-reliance *alongside* emotional literacy and relational intelligence, these wide-ranging capacities dovetail to create powerful and resilient human beings. Our children will be empowered to create vibrant friendships and communities they can rely on during challenging times. Ask any social anthropologist, this is literally what human beings are hardwired to do. Our survival as a species has always depended on our capacity for social connection.

Sadly, in American culture we seem to have lost sight of this seemingly obvious truth. We wrongly gender human capacities, doling out physicality to boys and men, and emotionality to girls and women. In order to make them "real men," our boys are shamed and punished for exhibiting any unwanted expression of emotion, trained to give the outward appearance that they are somehow immune to the vast catalogue of human insecurities, doubts and fears. The result is generations of emotionally isolated boys and men who hide their authentic selves behind what documentary director Jennifer Seibel Newsom calls "The Mask You Live In."

We Americans hold emotional connection as a female trait, rejecting it in our boys, demanding that they "man up" and adopt a strict regimen of emotional independence, even isolation, as proof they are real men. Behind the drumbeat message that real men are stoic and detached, is the brutal fist of homophobia, ready to crush any boy who might show too much of the wrong kind of emotions.

Meanwhile, the brutality with which we force men to conform to these rules, and the isolation that results, are creating epidemic levels of male depression, bullying, violence, addiction, illness, and suicide.

And there you have it, the key conclusions that almost ten years of thinking and writing about men's issues has led me to.

Remaking Manhood is a collection of my articles for The Good Men Project. Although not presented in strict chronological order, they do represent the evolution of my writing and my thinking. There are articles here which, with the passage of time, seem less fully representative of my thinking today. I leave them here more or less as they first appeared, with all their imperfections. If I have begun any journey, it has been from the more declarative towards the more nuanced, noting that in the end, I speak with absolute certainty for only one thing – that we must create and defend the widest possible range of options for how men can be men.

Being a writer for The Good Men Project has given me a powerful sense that something remarkable is happening, something remarkable that will some day be written about in history books in the same way that the women's rights movement is written about now.

What you hold in your hands is one writer's window into the global conversation about men. My stories are the product of my narrow social, cultural and generational context. I do not presume to define what other men should need or aspire to.

What I do advocate for is a more diverse masculinity, where men have the freedom to live more fulfilling and authentic lives, whatever those lives may look like. This fight for a wider ranging culture of masculinty across the intersectionalities of race, gender, sexual orientation, and culture is giving rise to violent tensions. It will not be an easy journey, but it is within these tensions that we evolve.

There are joyful stories to be told. Millions of men are raising their children, choosing personal satisfaction over profit, and seeking more egalitarian and sustainable relationships in which to live. For me, the global discussion about modern masculinity has been life changing.

Remaking Manhood is the result of endless hours of happy conversation with my wife and partner, Dr. Saliha Bava. She is as much responsible for *Remaking Manhood* as I am. Without her, this book would never have been written.

Saliha and I have now completed *The Relational Book for Parenting*. If *Remaking Manhood* is an effort to define what boys and men are up against, *The Relational Book for Parenting* represents our path forward to solutions. By exploring and growing our children's natural human capacities to form authentic, joyful relationships, we can change the world for the better while living happier and more fulfilling lives. If you would like to learn more about our new relational parenting book come to ThinkPlayPartners.com.

This conversation is only just beginning.

– Mark Greene, New York City, February 2018

The Lack of
Gentle Platonic Touch

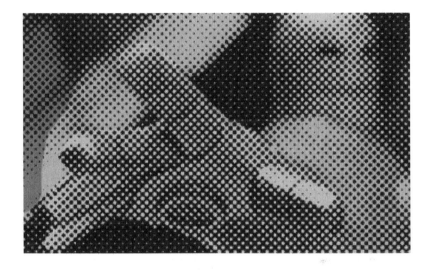

In American culture, we believe that men can never be entirely trusted in the realm of the physical. We collectively suspect that, given the opportunity, men will collapse into the sexual at a moment's notice. That men don't know how to physically connect otherwise. That men can't control themselves. That men are dogs.

There is no corresponding sexual narrative about women.

Accordingly, it has become every man's job to prove they can be trusted, in each and every interaction, day-by-day and case-by-case. In part, because so many men have behaved poorly. And so, we prove our trustworthiness by foregoing physical touch completely in any context in which even the slightest doubt about our intentions might arise. Which, sadly, is pretty much every context we encounter.

And where does this leave men? Physically and emotionally isolated. Cut off from the deeply human physical contact that is proven to reduce stress, encourage self-esteem and create community. Instead, we walk in the vast crowds of our cities alone in a desert of disconnection. Starving for physical connection.

We crave touch. We are cut off from it. The result is what I choose to call *touch isolation.*

How often do men actually get the opportunity to express affection through long-lasting, platonic touch? How often does it happen between men, or between men and women? Not a handshake or a hug, but lasting physical contact between two people that is comforting and personal but not sexual; between persons who are not lovers and never will be. Think: holding hands. Or leaning on each other. Sitting together. That sort of thing. Just the comfort of contact. And if you are a man, imagine five minutes of contact with another man. How quickly does that idea raise the ugly specter of homophobia? And why?

While women are much freer to engage in physical contact with each other, men remain suspect when they touch others. There is only one space in our culture where long-lasting, platonic physical contact is condoned for men, and that is between fathers and their very young children.

I found this kind of physical connection when my son was born. As a stay-at-home dad, I spent years with my son. Day after day, he sat in the crook of my arm, his little arm across my shoulder, his hand on the back of my neck.

As he surveyed the world from on high, I came to know a level of contentment and calm that had heretofore been missing in my life. The physical connection between us was so transformative that it changed my view of who I am and what my role is in the world. Yet it took having a child to bring this calming experience to me because so few other opportunities are possible to teach men the value and power of gentle, loving touch.

Unless it came in the form of roughhousing or unwelcome bullying, contact between myself and others simply didn't happen when I was a young child and teenager. My mother backed off from contact with me very early on, in part, I think, due to her upbringing. I can only guess that in her parents' house physical touch was something for toddlers but not for children past a certain age. Add to that the fact that my father was absent due to my parents' divorce and years of work overseas, and it meant I grew up without being held or touched.

This left me with huge insecurities about human contact. I was well into my twenties before I could put my arm around a girl I was dating without first getting drunk. To this day, I remain uncertain about where and how to approach contact with people, even those I consider close friends. It's not that I can't do it; it's just that it remains awkward, odd. As if we all feel like we're doing something slightly ... off?

Contact with male friends is always brief, a handshake, or a pat on the back. Hugs with men or women are a ballet of the awkward, a comedic choreography in which we turn our groins this way or that. Shoulders in, butts out, seeking to broadcast to anyone within line of sight that we are most certainly not having a sexual moment. We're working so hard to be seen as sexually neutral that we take no joy in these moments of physical connection.

Not only do we men distrust others in this muddled realm of physical touch – years of shaming and judgment have left us distrusting ourselves. Did I enjoy that too much? Am I having taboo thoughts? This distrust leaves us uncertain about touching another human being unless we have established very clear rules of engagement. Often, we give up and simply reduce those rules to being in a relationship. We allow ourselves long-lasting, comforting touch with our girlfriends or boyfriends. The vast universe of platonic human touch is suddenly reduced to the exclusive domain of one person and is blended into the sexual. That's a lot of need to put on one person, however loving and generous they might be.

Which leads to the question, how do we teach our sons to understand how touch works? How to parse out the sexual from the platonic? Is the pleasure of human contact inherently sexual to some degree? I doubt it's a question the average Italian man would ever ask himself. But here in America, generations of puritanical sexual shaming have made it a central question. By putting the fear of the sexual first in all our interactions, we have thrown out the baby with the bathwater, avoiding all contact rather than risk even the hint of unwanted sexual touch.

Many parents step back from physical contact with boys when their sons approach puberty. The contact these boys seek is often deemed confusing or even sexually suspect. And, most unbelievable of all, all opportunity for potential physical touch is abruptly handed over to young boys' female peers, who are suddenly expected to act as gatekeepers to touch; young girls who are no more prepared to take on this responsibility than boys are to hand it over.

And so, boys are cast adrift with two unspoken lessons:

1. All touch is sexually suspect.
2. Find a girlfriend or give up human contact.

A particularly damning message to boys who are gay.

American culture leaves boys few options. While aggression on the basketball court or bullying in the locker room often results in sporadic moments of human contact, gentleness likely does not. And young men, whose need for touch is channeled into physically rough interactions with other boys or fumbling sexual contact with girls, lose conscious awareness of the gentle, platonic contact of their own childhoods. Sometimes it's not until their children are born that they rediscover gentle, platonic touch; the holding and caring contact that is free from the drumbeat of sex, sex, sex that pervades our culture even as we simultaneously condemn it.

Is it any wonder that sexual relationships in our culture are so loaded with anger and fear? Boys are dumped on a desert island of physical isolation, and the only way they can find any comfort is to enter the blended space of sexual contact to get the connection they need. Which makes sexual relations a vastly more high stakes experience than it already should be. We encourage aggressive physical contact as an appropriate mode of contact for boys and turn a blind eye to bullying, even as we then expect them to work out some gentler mode of sexual contact in their romantic lives.

If men could diffuse their need for physical connection across a much wider set of platonic relationships, it would do wonders for our sense of connection in the world. As it is, we can't even manage a proper hug because we can't model what was never modeled for us.

We have seniors in retirement homes who are visited by dogs they can hold and pet. This does wonders for their health and emotional state of mind. It is due to the power of contact between living creatures. Why are good-hearted people driving around town, taking dogs to old folks homes? Because no one is touching these elderly people. They should have grandchildren in their laps every day, or a warm human hand to hold, not Pomeranians who come once a week. And yet, we put a dog in their laps instead of give them human touch, because we remain a culture that both values human contact and holds it highly suspect. We know the value of touch even as we do everything we can to shield ourselves from it.

American men have a tragic laundry list of reasons why we are not comfortable with touch.

1. We fear being labeled as sexually inappropriate by women.

2. We live in a virulently homophobic culture so any contact between men is suspect.
3. We don't want to risk any hint of being sexual toward children.
4. We don't want to risk our status as macho or authoritative by being physically gentle.
5. We don't ever want to deal with rejection when we reach out. (And in our touch-adverse culture that is the most likely outcome.)

But at the root of all these flawed rationalizations is the fact that most American men are never taught to do gentle non-sexual touch. Accordingly, the exact inappropriate, over-sexualized touch our society fears runs rampant, reinforcing our culture's self-fulfilling prophesy against men and touch. Meanwhile, this inability to comfortably connect via touch has left men emotionally isolated, contributing to rampant rates of alcoholism, depression and abuse.

And what if the lack of platonic touch is causing some men to be far too aggressive toward women, who, as the exclusive gatekeepers for gentle touch, are carrying a burden they could never hope to fully manage? Women, who arguably are both victims of and, in partnership with men, enforcers of the prohibition against platonic touch in American culture. Every single man, woman and child feels the impact of our collective touch phobia all across our society.

Brené Brown, in her groundbreaking TED Talk, "The Power of Vulnerability," (TED, 2011) speaks at length about the limitations men face when attempting to express vulnerability in our culture. She notes the degree to which men are boxed in by our culture's expectations about what a man is or is not allowed to do. I would suggest that the limitations placed on men extend to their physical expression though touch. And are just as damaging in that realm.

But here's the good news.

There are many reasons why full-time stay-at-home dads are proving to be such a transformative force in American culture. One powerful reason is the awakening of touch. As full-time dads, we are presented with the absolute necessity to hold our own wonderful children. We are learning about touch in the most powerful and life-affirming way; in ways that previous generations of men simply were not immersed in. Once you have held your sleeping child night after night or walked for years with their hand in yours, you are a changed person. You gain a fluency and confidence in touch that you will never lose. It is a gift to us men from our children that literally has the capacity to transform American culture.

Accordingly, now, when I am with a friend I do reach out. I do make contact. And I do so with confidence and joy. And I have my own clear path forward.

The patterns in my life may be somewhat set but I intend to do everything I can to remain in contact with my son in hopes that he will have a different view of touch in his life. I hug him and kiss him. We hold hands or I put my arm around him when we watch TV or walk on the street. I will not back off from him because someone somewhere might take issue with our physical connection. I will not back off because somehow there is an unspoken rule that I must cut him loose in the world to fend for himself. I hope we can hold hands even when he is a man. I hope we continue to hold hands until the day I die.

Ultimately, we will unlearn our fear of touch in the context of our personal lives and in our day-to-day interactions. Learning how to express platonic love and affection through touch is a vast and remarkable change that has to be lived. But it is so important that we do it, because it is central to having a rich, full life.

Touch is life.

For those who are interested, here are a few sources on the issues I raise here:

In an article in *Psychology Today*, Ray B. Williams writes about the central role of touch in living happier, healthier lives:

> Daniel Keltner, the founding director of the Greater Good Science Center and professor of psychology at University of California, Berkeley, says, "In recent years, a wave of studies has documented some incredible emotional and physical health benefits that come from touch. This research is suggesting that touch is truly fundamental to human communication, bonding, and health." Keltner cites the work of neuroscientist Edmund Ross, who found that physical touch activates the brain's orbitofrontal cortex, which is linked to feelings of reward and compassion. Keltner contends that 'studies show that touch signals safety and trust, it soothes. It activates the body's vagus nerve, which is intimately involved with our compassion response ...

A clear indication of how central touch is in our emotional and cognitive development can be seen in the range of studies examining touch and infants (both human and animal), here summarized in an article titled "The Importance of Touch in Development," found on the National Center for Biotechnology Information's website (www.ncbi.nlm.nih.gov/pmc/articles/PMC2865952). The article notes:

> Developmental delay is often seen in children receiving inadequate or inappropriate sensory stimulation. For example, orphaned infants exposed to the bleakest of conditions in eastern European institutions exhibited impaired growth and cognitive development, as well as an elevated incidence of serious infections and attachment disorders. Much evidence

now points to the importance of touch in child development and suggests the possibility that these orphaned infants are not suffering from maternal deprivation, per se, but from sensory deprivation, and more specifically a deprivation of mechanosensory stimulation.

Boys and Self-loathing

As a kid, I was so full of fear and self-doubt that it resulted in my feeling physically sick a dozen times a day. Confusion about how I should behave and disgust with who I was would wash over me, creating a prickling sensation that raced across my skin, resolving into a physical pain in my chest. It was like being shocked or hit. It happened whenever I interacted with others or even *imagined* myself interacting with others.

The roots of my self-loathing were both circumstantial and biological. They included my parents' acrimonious divorce, an absent father, an explosively volatile and physically abusive older brother, a jarring relocation and a very late puberty. But events alone are not what hold a child back. It was the lack of communication about these events. It was the silence.

I grew up in a time when talking to your kids about their feelings was about as likely as their dancing with the Bolshoi Ballet. My parents were born during the Great Depression. My childhood was a cakewalk compared to what they had to endure. My father's stories are a powerful evocation of grit and resiliency. I don't think he had a lot of conversations with anyone as a child about how he was feeling; the blinding white flash of the back of his stepfather's hand, yes, but not a lot of chitchat.

So, he and my mother took us as far as they could. And as much as I respect their journeys, mine is not made invalid by comparison. My belief in the need for communication is more than just wanting something better for my son. There is a larger truth at work here. On a meta level, we all simply cannot live good lives without connection and communication. The central role of communication in parenting is that it helps children and parents process and frame the joys and challenges in our lives.

As a child, I needed help to parse the complexity of the world. I needed to talk to someone who could help me make sense of things. Instead, I was left to construct a worldview on my own. This is not a job any 8-year-old should have to do alone. And there was little time for that, anyway. I spent most of my time tracking the kids who were a direct threat to me.

My strategy for creating safety was to play the feisty little guy. I took up smoking at twelve. I brown-nosed the bigger guys on my block. I always had a compliment for them. I was always ready to give them a cigarette. I formed what alliances I could. At one point, I landed a free-period job working in the assistant principal's office. His name was Mr. Wooten; a tall, grim man who walked with a limp. Someone said he had suffered polio as a child. From an educational perspective, he was not the carrot. He was the stick.

When the school toughs would get sent in for misbehaving, I would stamp their forms and send them back to class, without their ever having to visit Mr. Wooten. Before they left, I would open the confiscation drawer in the big, grey file cabinet and hand them a pack of cigarettes and a lighter.

This bought me some immunity during recess, in those terrible moments when the bullies would scan the ranks of the smaller kids and pick the guy who was going to take the beatdown. Luckily for me, I had some sense of style. There were a number of boys who simply didn't get it – a guy named Edward quite literally had a pocket protector and a slide rule. I recall deep pangs of sympathy as savage abuse rained down on him. He was like the cow that was driven in downstream from the herd to attract the piranhas. They would close in on him in the dark corner of the locker room as the rest of us squirmed past to the relative safety of the well-lit gymnasium. I always felt sick with guilt that he was back there, wide-eyed and supremely puzzled behind the wall of thick bodies. To this day, my gut boils at the thought that no one in the school administration gave a shit about Edward.

But to save my own skin I was happy to scoff at Edward as loudly as the rest. To make him the butt of the kind of vicious jokes that leave you feeling filthy forty years later. To push him in downstream and race across the river. Edward and Larry and Jack and all the rest who haunted the nearly abandoned chess club were sacrificial sheep to the young alpha adherents of directionless masculine savagery.

I got myself elected to the student council by drawing endless election posters. My opponent was a girl named Louise Bone. My opponent's polite drawings of her name and the word "elect" (I'm thinking maybe she included some flowers?) took a back seat to my drawings of a grinning dog with a bone in its sharp teeth.

I can only imagine what it was like for her to see my posters making fun of her name all over the school. It would not surprise me if the phrase "Don't pull a boner" was invoked. I don't recall. For me, getting elected was my ticket to getting out of P.E. for the final year of school, and I didn't care who went down in order for me to escape that place. My caustic campaign struck a chord with my peers. I was elected.

The first girl who ever agreed to be my girlfriend was named Anne; initiated by the delivery of the words, "Would you go with me?" scrawled in my nervous hand on a piece of lined notebook paper. Anne was on the student council with me. So, we decided to form an alliance; to become boyfriend and girlfriend. We sat together at lunch and passed notes. We did not kiss. We did not hold hands. We simply assigned each other the titles and were therefore free of the stigma of not being with anyone.

I had no sexual urges to speak of. I was still physically a child. Puberty was a year or more away. I recall the physical agony it caused me to try and give Anne a kiss on the cheek. All I had to do was lean over in an unguarded moment and give her a little peck. I knew that this was necessary. I knew I needed to validate my role as the boy. The pressure to do so was almost unbearable. But I could not do it.

No matter how hard I tried, simply reaching out and touching her was impossible. The best I could manage was brushing the back of my hand against hers as we walked; an accidental touch. But kiss her? Impossible. As if in order to lean over to her, I would be pulling against some massive personal horror bolted firmly to every failure I had ever experienced. I knew that kids my age were rolling around on this one particular sweaty mattress in this one particular neighborhood garage. Feeling what, in god's name, I couldn't have guessed.

When it became clear to us that neither Anne nor I were inclined to fumble around in the alarming realm of physicality, I was left feeling like a relieved failure. It ate at me because of all the bragging sexual dialogues swirling about. I didn't want sex. But I wanted to be able to brag about it to someone. Anyone.

Once, toward the end of my painfully courteous relationship with Anne, we were sitting side by side in the lunchroom. My older brother took up a position facing us at a nearby table. He spoke to his buddy in a loud voice about how I couldn't even bring myself to touch my girlfriend. He carried on loudly so that kids for tables around could clearly hear him.

In that moment, I fought to reach across and simply touch Anne. On the shoulder, or arm or hand. I couldn't do it. I was acutely aware that I simply didn't care to, making my inability to touch Anne embarrassing as both a prospective lie and a failure of manhood in the same moment. Shame flooded my face red. And hatred. I can still remember my brother laughing. "See?" he kept saying over and over. "See?"

By the first year of high school, I had only barely entered puberty. I was years behind my peers in qualifying for the attention of girls. My voice was still quite high. I giggled hysterically. When I discovered beer, I drank and then poured out a ceaseless stream of self-pity stories. Girls walked off in droves. It took ten years to get myself on track, to build any kind of baseline of self-esteem. And learning to forgive myself for not doing better as a sad and frightened 8-year-old somehow remains an ongoing process.

We internalize the negative messages we get as children. When we hear them in our adult relationships they seem so familiar that we let them slip in again. It's a cycle of grief and pain that can only be broken through human communication and thoughtful self-care.

But I will say this to men and women alike. You can't let other people tell your stories for you, or censor you, or shame you. If you get a hint of that from someone who purports to care about you, go somewhere and rethink that relationship. Immediately. And if it continues long term, leave for good. And don't bother looking back.

Being deeply unhappy, even in the past, is not a story men are encouraged to share. When we talk about what has happened to us, we feel pressure to construct a narrative that eventually has us overcoming our troubles. It's embarrassing to admit that we're not done with our old business. That old slights and old wounds still pain us, sometimes more deeply than we can express. But men need to grieve what has been lost. We need to advocate proudly for our right to grieve; because honestly, many of us have never had our funerals. We never have been granted the retelling of our lost battles and weary retreats, and because of this, they remain with us, long after they should have been dead and buried.

To tell our stories of grief is to be vulnerable. And vulnerability is the third rail of male expression. Put simply, to go there can get you erased, rejected, expelled. While there is a popular assumption that women are asking for us to connect in more emotional ways, our intimate partners can often be repelled by male vulnerability. This is because there are so few spaces in which vulnerability is framed as an asset, as a pathway to strength; so few spaces where it is even visible at all. So, on some level our partners cannot be blamed for turning away from displays of vulnerability. But vulnerability is the key to living a fuller life.

Whenever I see an aggressive man, I see a man who is taking with force what he cannot devise a way to freely offer. It is the opposite of being vulnerable. While there is ample evidence that our human side, our stories and our vulnerability can create more significant connections in our lives, we, as men, often hide because we have seen those who rely on us for strength withdrawing at signs of uncertainty or, worse, sadness. So, we struggle as men with the double bind. To be expressive can heal our souls, to be vulnerable can open up the doors of self-awareness, but society and often our most intimate partners are not prepared for those dialogues because they can be immense.

More than once I have been asked the following question about my writing. "What do you think about your son or his friends reading this?"

It is a complex question. At what age? I don't think I want him reading it in the next five minutes, but are we all to hide our stories until our children are grown? Stories that I believe add in crucial ways to the changing ideas about what it is to be a man? Are we all to hide our stories generationally? To be released a half-century later like some declassified Cold War documents splattered with redacted details meant to protect still virulent state secrets?

Silence is shaming. Inherent in the call for keeping our stories private is the assumption that we should be ashamed of them.

Brené Brown, in her TED talk, "The Power of Vulnerability," notes that people have a simple fear – that if people find out enough about us, we will not be worthy of connection. She goes on to say, though, that the happiest people she has met prioritize vulnerability and authenticity. Brown writes, "Vulnerability sounds like truth and feels like courage. Truth and courage aren't always comfortable, but they're never weakness."

We live in a society that asks man to whitewash their narratives and keep a lid on their emotions. The varied and rich personal stories of men and women and the conversations those stories evoke are part of the greater narrative of being human. If we are struggling in life, it is not because we have shared too many stories. It is because we have shared too few.

And then there is this: our children are creating their stories right now. They are parsing out meaning and creating the frames that will define their view of the world and of themselves. How can we, as parents, invite them to share those stories with us? How can we help them develop rich, complex conceptual skills, such as creating multiple frames for any challenges they may be facing? How can we help them feel safe, confident and, most of all, free to share their experience of the world?

The telling of stories and the conversations that result create powerful intergenerational connections. Our kids need for us to hear their stories and engage them in conversations about life and living. It is in the sharing of our stories that our sons and daughters will find the confidence and the courage to live authentic and fulfilling lives.

Please note: The names here have been changed to protect the individuals in my past. My recollections and my interpretations are my own.

Cruelty, Perversion and the Boy Scouts

I was twelve when I joined the Boy Scouts. I lasted about 18 months. I got a few merit badges. I went camping. I played capture the flag. I was not particularly inspired by Scouting. I remained a Tenderfoot until I quit.

My recollections are pretty hazy. There is a lot of information I simply couldn't supply if you asked me. What was my troop number? Was my brother in the same patrol I was? Which kids from my school were there? For how long? Sorry, mostly hazy.

The faces and names that do come back to me from Scouting are those tied directly to acts of cruelty or violence. My memories of those moments are quite clear.

Many of the kids in my troop also went to my junior high school. Coming in, we already had our places in the pecking order. We already knew where we stood. The difference was that we were in closer proximity to older boys, some of whom were four or five years our seniors. In Scouts, unlike school, there wasn't the vast population of other students to hide among. We were isolated with these boys.

I first went to my first overnight Scout camp in the middle of summer. Each patrol in our Scout troop had been assigned a campsite. We were to haul our packs in and get set up. We had only been there for a few hours when it started. The largest boys came racing though the campsites. There were five or six of them. They would spot a target, tackle him in the dirt, pin his arms and legs, pull up his shirt, and start slapping his stomach good and hard, a dozen or more times. The boy would scream and thrash under the assault. Often tears would come. The uproar echoed through the quiet woods. It is not possible that the Scoutmasters couldn't have heard this. It hit me like an electric shock. The Scoutmasters were not coming to put an end to it. This was one of our troop's rituals. Somewhere back along the trail, our Scoutmasters were calmly setting up camp. They approved of slapping a boy's stomach until it turned an angry pink color. Giving pink bellies, they called it.

Each kid did his own survival calculations in the moment the pink bellies started. Some raced in to attack the victims, hoping to align themselves with the aggressors. This rarely worked. Their turns came soon enough. Others stood rooted to the spot, sickly half smiles on their faces, preferring to take their pain up front than to be hunted over the length of the afternoon. "Maybe it'll be less bad," they might have thought, "if I don't make them look for me." It wasn't. They weren't taking into account the raging contempt for weakness inherent in actions of your garden-variety teenage sadist. Those who offered themselves up willingly took savage beatings. Passivity only inflamed the cruelty and contempt that drove the entire exercise.

For two seconds I stared, like a shocked pedestrian watching a bank robbery spill out onto a noontime city street. Then I dropped my pack and took off running, making a beeline into the woods away from the campsites. I stayed away from camp until late in the afternoon, sitting on a log, fighting a combination of prickly fear and disgusted boredom.

I recall how uniform and dull the woods were. Mostly scraggly, new-growth pine trees and poison ivy as far as the eye could see. Somewhere, Boy Scouts were camping in the inspiring grandeur of Yosemite Park, but not us. We were in the pinewoods of east Texas, where only the mosquitoes were seeing anything that inspired them.

Eventually, I made my way back into the quiet campsite. The storm had passed. This was day one of my introduction to Scout camping. Where capture the flag could drift off course into Lord of the Flies at a moment's notice. All of it stank of overheated sour sweat and fear.

A Scout is Trustworthy, Loyal, Helpful, Friendly, Courteous, Kind ...

This is the insidious impact of bullying on children. It becomes the primary filter for their experience of the world. What might have been a vibrant, exciting week at a wonderful camp becomes instead a deadening scramble to avoid eye contact, proximity and exposure. When bullying takes root, engagement, high ideals, learning, hope and self-esteem fall by the wayside. They cease to have relevancy. The full focus of a child's world becomes when and where a stranger's angry, sweaty hands will be put on them, day after day after day.

How victims experienced their abuse very clearly reflected each individual's relative social status and level of self-esteem. Was their moment of being abused an acknowledgement of their promise as a rising member of the group? Or was it a reinforcement of their otherness, their lack of access going forward? It was case by case. But the abuse rarely varied. It was how the victim interpreted these acts, coupled with whether or not they also participated in the abuse of others, that fully informed their experience of it. The smaller kids among us obviously didn't take it well at all. We weren't being initiated. We were just being brutalized. We were the victims of a simple chronological joke. The punch line was puberty. Over and over again.

We attended our Scout meetings at the local Presbyterian Church one evening a week. Thursday evenings, I think. This was the same church my mother and stepfather took me to every Sunday. It didn't help that our church was already ground zero for emotionally vacant, intellectually vacuous, spiritual malaise. The church's "fellowship hall" was a large wood paneled basketball court. We had our assigned places to stand, grouped by patrols. I can't recall who was in my patrol.

Roughhousing is one of the social currencies of boyhood. Typically, boys do wrestle, kick and so on. In the group of boys from our street, there was a range of physical size, economic status, and social aptitude. We were all about the same age, but we were very different in terms of our status in the world. The alpha boys wrestled those boys who were on the next rung down, who wrestled the littlest of us. But on our street, the roughhousing was among boys who had spent long years together. There was some honest friendship mixed in. And most importantly, I often saw real restraint from those guys. As a smaller kid, I was rarely pushed around unless I initiated it.

But Scouting was different. Like school, it incorporated aggression from strangers to strangers. There existed the idea that the bigger kids could lay hands on anyone they wanted to. The crazy part is, we all accepted it. We all *expected* it. We thought it was normal. That was just being a kid in those days. As the father of an 8-year-old boy, I am working to ensure that being a kid is different now. But in case it isn't, my son is in karate.

In Scouting, you move up in the ranks by mastering skills and earning merit badges. It was at camp that we held the ceremonies by which our accomplishments were acknowledged and we advanced. Part of this advancement process was initiations. On one night, all those in the troop who were advancing, as well as those of us who had failed to advance, would undergo individual initiations created by the older campers and Scoutmasters.

My initiation was fairly lackluster. I have written before about my strategies for avoiding being a victim. But some of the younger guys in our troop took a real pounding. And as much as I sympathized with them, I left them to their fate. I understood them to be so intensely awkward that any association with them could have rubbed off on me with catastrophic results.

Take Hayward for instance; the boy whose earnest, pseudo-military enthusiasm for Scouts was beaten down in short order. Hayward's uniform was ironed. His pants literally had a crease. He wore that uniform with pride, his shirt tucked in neatly, his collar buttoned up smartly. Hayward had a huge forehead. There are no two ways around it, the guy's forehead was massive. When he dropped those horn-rimmed glasses on the brim of his nose, the collective effect was equivalent to a blinking neon sign that said, "Please make my life a living hell."

Personally, I always liked Hayward. He had an open, earnest quality. He was a chess club kid. He meant no one any harm. Hayward and I shared some similar challenges. Like his mom, my mother was hell-bent on making me into a punching bag at school. She insisted I have a burr haircut, something which would be quite stylish in current hip-hop circles but which, back then, was the kiss of death. But she didn't end her efforts there. During a time when most kid's blue jeans had holes in the knees, she took mine, cut them off above the knees, and hemmed them neatly. I was at severe risk for being confused with Little Lord Fauntleroy. Each day was a frantic exercise in trying to undo her work on the way to school. Untucking my shirt. Hanging a cigarette on my bottom lip. Anything I could do to not look like a primary target.

Hayward wasn't so adaptable.

The night of Hayward's initiation, I heard him screaming somewhere off in the woods. It was the sound a trapped, terrified animal makes. I was not witness to what happened, but I saw him later at the cold outdoor showers where he stood well past midnight trying to wash himself clean. I found out then what they had done to him.

They had taken Hayward into the woods and made him strip

down. In the beam of a flashlight, they showed him an ant bed on the ground at his feet. They *knew* he was allergic to ant bites. They stirred up the ant bed. These were red fire ants whose sting is extremely painful. They blindfolded Hayward. They threw dirt on him and began poking him with handfuls of pine needles. He didn't know it was pine needles. He thought he was covered in red ants. He began screaming.

On another campout they stripped Hayward down and covered him in peanut butter. It was late fall. It took Hayward most of the night to wash it off in the cold showers. I recall some guys were there with him, keeping him company. It was too much for any of us to just ignore. It was too cruel. I wish I could remember who was there with him. I would name them and thank them here. But I don't remember. I don't think I stayed long; again, probably for fear of attracting collateral damage. My plight was too similar to Hayward's. But I remember seeing him the next morning, his pale skin fiery red and raw from hours of scrubbing. He was exhausted. His eyes hollow. Within a day or so he regained his plucky cheerfulness, but that night likely stayed with him. Maybe he thought Scouts would be different with all the talk about honor, kindness, country, reverence and god. Too bad it was all bullshit.

And then there was Randy. He was our age. He was one of the good-looking, confident kids. He had charm and size and was one of those kids who never lacked for something to say or somewhere to go next. He eventually ended up on the football team. He eventually ended up with the tall blonde wife and the two heart attacks.

Randy's initiation comes back to me very clearly because I was right there watching. I was looking right down on him as a crowd of boys pinned him down, yanked down his underwear and broke a raw egg over his exposed genitals in the midday sun. I kid you not. Now, I definitely didn't help pin him down and I certainly had no idea what they were going to do until the raw egg appeared and his pants came down. It was shocking to me. I can still see the raw egg running across Randy's naked skin.

As I recall, Randy took it all in stride. Another kid would have been humiliated, but not Randy. By all appearances, he viewed it as a sign of his status that such a wildly ambitious and crazy initiation was cooked up just for him. Maybe I'm wrong about this, but that's the impression I was left with. If I'm wrong, Randy, I'm sorry. But you were one emotionally tough kid.

I honestly do not know what part of being a man feeds into the cruel cycle of initiations that dominate some male organizations. To this day, university fraternities continue to conduct initiations that get hopeful, socially needy young men killed. (Want a shock? Do a Google search.) Young men die trying to drink two quarts of gin locked in the trunk of a car, or smother as the sides of a grave collapse in on them while they lie naked and shivering in the bottom, looking up at the senior members of their would-be brotherhood. Less ritualized initiations take place daily in the good old boy clubs of corporations and public institutions, where dishing out cruelty is meant to somehow validate men as creatures who can "take it."

Take it. Is that what men were born to do? Take it? If so, we are a doomed species, slogging our way through systems and organizations of our own creation that require we suffer at the hands of those who came before us so that those who come after can suffer at ours. What is it about being a man that so easily embraces this kind of vicious institutionalized cruelty? What is it about being a man that we allow this kind of ritualized abuse to continue to this day? Why do some men express their power by abusing those weaker than them? When, in fact, weakness should be defined as the need to abuse anyone ever, at any time.

I realize that women can and do commit acts of cruelty. But as a boy, I did not fear girls. I did not fear women. I feared boys and men. They were the threats I had to track each and every day. They were the reason I had to hide and run and fight and fear. It was them. As a man and a father, I am committed to putting an end to bullying in all its forms. We're better than this. Our sons are better than this.

As for my initiation? Oh, yeah. Well, as I said, that was pretty lackluster. I was taken out in the dark woods, blindfolded and made to sit. They pissed a ring around me and told me not to move. When their footsteps had faded away, I took off my blindfold and walked back to camp.

Scout's honor.

The Last Late Show with My Father

My father left when I was six years old. The age my son is now. I don't remember my father leaving. Did he walk out with a suitcase? Did they engineer it so he left while we were at school? I remember an argument, in the back bedroom with the door closed. I remember doing my little-child Saturday chores as the spring wind blew through the house. I remember that. But his exit, days or weeks afterward, is not something I recall, forty-five years later. I don't remember a day when he was suddenly gone.

There are things I do recall about my father. And I have the luxury of knowing where and when they happened because within a year or so, my mother remarried and we moved away. The house where I knew my father as the man married to my mother, where I stood as a small child looking up at him, is gone to the place of dreams. Of memories that form themselves into long rafts of lost emotions. A place where, if I am lucky, I will go when I die. I want to go there into that sunny backyard again and be ready to run to him when he calls.

I still remember looking out the back window of the car as we drove away for the last time from the house I was born into, its garage door gaping open for some reason; the garage light still on as dusk fell. The freezer where I had gotten my frozen Tupperware ice pops, standing open. That can't be right. Why would we have left the garage open? Exposed to the world? Perhaps this memory is false. Based on what I knew to be in the garage instead of what was actually in my line of sight that summer evening. But the moment of deep loss, looking out the back window as the house receded and disappeared, is the truth. Regardless of what, exactly, peoples the landscape.

I recall missing my father as the years passed. I recall missing him so much I thought I would simply give up and die. The missing was a vast blank space of yearning, of wanting his touch and his smell, a loss so big, so huge, that I was lost in it for years. I remember a scratchy call from overseas from him one Christmas that we kids waited up hours for. I remember how empty that call was.

When children are forced to release something they hold dear, it cements into their memories the moments preceding it; the way of the world before that change. The smells and sounds. They hold onto what is gone with a feverish intensity. When a child loses someone or someplace dear to them, you had best be ready to replace it with something warm and real, or you will haunt your child with loss.

Before he left, my father would sit up nights watching TV. My mother usually went to bed early, exhausted by the work of raising four children. She was unable to find the energy to be present with her husband after her children went to sleep. My father watched TV alone. My bedroom was just down the long, straight hall. I shared it with my brother.

My brother was a sleeper. I was a listener. There in my bed, I listened to the house growing quiet as my older sisters were put to bed. As my mother retired. Until my father sat alone watching TV. Some nights, my father would get up and make a milkshake. I could hear the blender in the kitchen. It would shut off and then, rising on bare feet I would go to the bedroom door, careful not to wake my brother. I would ever so carefully open the door and peek around the edge of the doorframe.

There, down the hallway, he sat on the couch, a lamp beyond him, the warm glow backlighting him. And to this day I can see the warm glow there. I can see his silhouette. And as I peeked out, silent, he would turn and he would gesture to me. Then, I would enter the hall, quietly close the door, and race up the hall to join him on the couch.

There it would sit on the side table next to him. The extra glass. The extra vanilla milkshake for me to sip, as I nuzzled in under his arm to watch TV.

In Houston, in 1966, they had this program called "The Late Show." It wasn't a national show. It was a local. It came on after the news. I think it was on channel 11. They showed old black-and-white movies. And as the show began, "The Late Show" artwork popped up and a jingle played. The jingle went like this:

The Late Show,
Nothing could be finer than The Late Show.
Nothing could be greater than the greatest of stars,
Right on your own TV.

Those moments with my father carried me through some very dark times. He loved me. His warmth and his charm weren't enough to quell the demons that wrecked his marriage, but he left me with a sense that I was special, and that I was loved. Even now, when I sit with my son, after a divorce and after moving him out of the house he was born into, I remember the lesson my father taught me. That the love of a father can heal wounds; heal the emptiness of loss. Even when that very love itself is what is lost.

And so, I hold my son close. I'm not leaving him. I'm with him. And I try to remember to be the man on the couch that wants him to peek out his door. And I think back to my father, young and strong and full of confusion; still finding a moment for me.

On the couch as "The Late Show" began, there was a black-

and-white graphic of a city with a big moon above it; a magical city where my father and I sat drinking our milkshakes. I felt in those moments, leaning against my father, that the world couldn't be more perfect. It's funny that all these years later, I can still sing that song. I still can see down into that glass, where the vanilla milkshake floated in chunks.

But I can't see him leaving.

Babies and the Rebirth of Men

I had my son when I was 45 years old. We draw together and we walk home from school in the afternoons. I can still manage a competent game of kickball at the park with six or eight kids swarming around. I sometimes wonder about the way my life was before my son was born. Did I really have that much time in the day? Why didn't I get more done in 45 years? Really, what kind of an idiot was I?

Adults without kids are free to create their own patterns for living. Yes, they have jobs and yes, they have in-laws, but these influences are not pattern wrecking. They are pattern adjusting. The illusion of control over one's life remains intact.

Adults with babies are a whole different ball of wax. Raising babies, especially full time, inexorably forces you to dump your long-held patterns, the ways of living your life that you think matter so very, very much. The ways in which you validate yourself. The methods through which you handle stress. The people you spend time with. Even right down to what you see in the mirror.

Caring for babies doesn't make you change these patterns, it blows them to pieces. When my wife and I were pregnant, a lot of other parents told us our lives were REALLY, REALLY, REALLY going to change. They told us this with this manic tone. It bordered on Shakespearean in its dark intensity. As if we were already doomed. Our fates decided. The die cast. And of course, they were right. This version of me that stood around at some party chatting away, 39 days away from a long night of ice chips and labor, really was doomed. I was living my last days; about to be replaced by a totally different person.

No doubt, I had some kind of carefully designed pattern for

living my life before my son came. Some strategy for being a person. Whatever that was, it is long gone. Levered out of the way by a tool so powerful no force on earth can resist it. Once the baby came, those old patterns I had designed for myself were about as useless as the birthing music CD I had made, thinking that the Debussy would be helpful. It wasn't helpful. It never even got played.

For most of us men, here's how it goes. When the baby first arrives in your life, you take a big breath and you start getting things done. It's a natural response. As a man, you make sense of a new baby's arrival in the same way you might deal with a new job. You continue washing and fixing and painting and buying and doing a list of stuff. Typically, the mother is caring for the baby. This is, in part, because a child emerges from his mother's body and enters her arms. Furthermore, an infant in the first weeks of life sleeps, as does his or her mother. A father goes about the business of making sure the sleeping is supported. During the first weeks, the baby creates some demands on the father, but they are not emotional, they are logistical. Tasks are easy. Tasks are even satisfying. Tasks don't change who you are.

But then comes a fork in the road. A spiritual and personal transition that saunters up while you're fixing the screen door, taps you on the shoulder and says, "Guess what? You're dead. The you that's right here, right now, fixing this screen door? Buh-bye. It's time for the new you."

And you respond, "The hell you say. I ain't going nowhere. You see this Phillips-head screwdriver here? You see this door hinge? Get real. I survived my parents. I can survive this."

And the spiritual transition smiles and says, "Sweetie, you didn't survive your parents. They survived you."

And then your spouse drops a 6-week-old baby in your arms and goes to the store. You hear the front door close. The car starts and she's gone for the afternoon. And you realize that the baby sleeping any more. That comfortable list of dad tasks is now yesterday's news. The practical shifts to the personal. A human being is right there. Awake. Looking at you.

I can't speak for other dads, but it scared the crap out of me. I remember holding my son and feeling like the clock had screeched to a halt. When will my wife be back? When will I be able to get to work on painting the porch? I felt as if I was literally tearing in half. Part of me was willing to work twenty hours a day if someone would just take the baby away and let me keep doing things MY WAY.

I wasn't ready to be with a baby. I didn't understand the rhythm of it. What was the beginning, middle, and end of this task? Every story of my childhood swarmed over me. Every loss. Every failing. Life seemed inexorably sad in that moment, alone in the house with my newborn son. "What the hell is WRONG WITH ME?" I thought, my fears lurching up. I felt utterly trapped, but looking back, I can see why it was scary. This fear was about things that could not be negotiated away, or run from, or laughed off. This fear was about taking on a task that could never ever be completed.

My problem was, I really didn't know how to be still, to just sit still and be with him. Whatever your strengths might be, babies will always need something you didn't naturally arrive with, because basically they need everything. And they need it for years. It's like staring down a long hallway with no exits and only one path forward. And in that moment, you recall all the stories of parents who didn't so much walk that long hallway, as stumble screaming down it. Spanking and yelling and cursing and drinking their way into divorce court and child support and uncomfortable dinners with a 20-year-old kid they had never come to know.

"Am I that guy?" you ask yourself.

At which point, you either bail out or you start changing. And yes, you can bail out and hold on to the patterns of living you had created for yourself long ago. You can choose to defend them to the death. Men and women do it all the time. Sometimes they physically walk out the door. Sometimes they just check out emotionally, leaving behind an automaton of a parent who goes through the motions with some secret part of themselves locked away for twenty years. Those folks do not make the change that parenting demands. Those fierce souls go another, lonelier way. And they never come to know their children.

I like to think I made the changes. Or more accurately, they made me.

If you let parenting lead you into new ways of being outside your well-worn comfort zone, you will find growth. You learn patience. You learn to let things be uncertain. You learn to say yes, instead of no. You re-learn how to play. You give up control (and thereby gain a bit of it). You experience the point at which physical and emotional exhaustion makes fingertip-to-fingertip contact with the divine.

Clear memories come back to me of my son's first couple of years. Two of those memories are with me now. One is that fearful moment of first being left alone with him. But I have a second memory as well. I recall walking through my house at bedtime with my infant son in my arms, his little head on my shoulder, his little body light as a feather. It is dark and my living room is lit by only a nightlight. His mother is resting upstairs. I am walking him in slow circles, my steps punctuated by the soft creaking of the wooden floor.

My son is not crying. He rarely ever did. He is happy. He is just breathing and moving a little; settling in my arms. As I am walking, I am murmuring a song. "You Are My Sunshine ... " I have changed one word of the lyrics to make sure he knows how I feel. As I walk holding him, I am utterly content and at peace. Walking with him this way at bedtime was one of the rituals that had evolved between us. The quiet of the house; the gentle creaking of the floor as I made slow circles.

At some magical point between the first time I was left alone with him, and this moment, as I held him close in the darkened house, who I was and how I viewed my place in the world had changed. The process was terribly difficult. Many times, I had struggled in ways that were no doubt painful to watch. It took time to learn the power of yes and the liberation that comes with giving yourself over to the little, tiny needs of the moment. The little needs that come one after another after another. But I was in the moment now, circling the floor with my dozing son. I was in the zone and I was truly home, possibly for the first time in my life. And as my son drifted off to sleep, his breathing changing to the sleep rhythm I know so well, I murmured my song to him.

You are my sunshine,
My only sunshine,
You make me happy,
When skies are gray.

You'll *always* know dear,
How much I love you.
Please don't take
My sunshine away.

The opportunity to open up my life to my son continues to change the person that I am, even as he grows and moves out into the world, and eventually away from me. In caring for him and looking after his littlest needs, I have set my feet on a path that has taught me things about myself I would never have known without him. It is a complex process full of dark moments and frustrations. Ask any parent. It's the tearing down of who you were and the giving over to service and change. It is not a journey for the weak of heart. When I see a mother or a dad collapsed beyond

42

exhaustion on a park bench staring blankly at their kids, I know how they feel. But the process of really engaging in my son's life for the last six years has taught me one thing that I will never forget.

That who I am inside the boundaries of myself is only a small part of who I really am. I am defined by what I create in the world in relationship with my son, with my wife, and with others. It's a lesson that was a long time coming. As men, we can learn this through service to our children and the purposeful setting aside of our own needs. We learn it in the baptism of birth and the long nights and days of care and attention.

As babies grow, so do we.

Men as Providers

The conversation about men is accelerating exponentially. It is happening, in large part, because of groundbreaking dialogues that were born in the women's rights movement.

Women's rights dialogues have normalized the following idea: that men and women should consciously reflect on our idea of self, but also about the social and cultural contexts from which these ideas emerge. And if, in a culture of haves and have nots, we view ourselves as oppressed by virtue of our class, gender, race, religion, or economic status, this process of self-reflection encourages us to better understand our own unknowing complicity in the systems of oppression. If we are subjugated, it comes in part through the stories and ideas we have unknowingly internalized.

For generations now, the women's movement has focused on awakening these kinds of internal dialogues in women within the context of a male-dominated society. In asking women to examine their internal dialogues, the women's movement has awoken a more universal view of social justice in women and successfully driven increasing legal and institutional parity for women and other disempowered groups.

The movement toward universal equality is a good thing. Decency and justice requires nothing less of us. Yet, even as women and minorities continue to make progress towards parity, men are only just now publicly confronting the oppressive cultural restrictions that have come to be known as the Man Box.

The Man Box is a set of rigid expectations that define what a "real man" is, particularly in American culture. A real man is strong and stoic. He doesn't show emotions other than anger and excitement. He is a breadwinner. He is heterosexual. He is able-bodied. He plays or watches sports. He is the dominant participant in every exchange. He is a firefighter, a lawyer, a CEO. He is a man's man. This "real man," as defined by the Man Box, represents what is supposedly normative and acceptable within the tightly controlled performance of American male masculinity.

One value central to the Man Box is the expectation that men are to earn money and support their families. While seemingly benign, this expectation is rooted in a time when only men could be employed and therefore only men wielded the economic power in the home.

Accordingly, what the Man Box offered was simple. "Do what you are told on the factory floor, be the undisputed king in your home." Men, by retaining control of their family's economic survival, held vast amounts of authority within the family structure; authority which often resulted in the brutal oppression of their wives and children. It was the devil's bargain of economic power for American men; a devil's bargain that is fading away as women become increasingly economically independent. But the ghost of it remains.

Before all else, men are expected to be good providers. Our parent's generation expects it of us, the family courts expect it of us, women on first dates often expect it, and in the event of an early death, our life insurance policies presuppose it. The simple mechanics of being a good provider excludes men from a number of other spaces that, not coincidentally, are reserved for women. What's more, as they aspire to switch traditional breadwinner roles with men in our evolving economy, even highly successful professional women collapse into the expectation that men are supposed to provide.

Imagine a woman saying the following: "I want to stay home and care for my child while my husband works." This is universally accepted as a valid expression of gender for women. Although it is challenging to maintain a single-income household given the economic pressures of modern life, the idea of a stay-at-home mom is encouraged, even heartwarming.

Now picture a man saying: "I want to stay home and care for my child while my wife works." And let's be clear. For the purposes of this example, the man is not saying this because of some external factor. He is not unemployed or laid off. He is not on a lower-paying career path than his wife. He is simply saying that he wants to be a full-time parent to his children, and he wants his wife to pay the bills so that he can stay in the home and raise them. This is what he wants.

This image generates a significant degree of cognitive dissonance, even for a fully-engaged parent like myself. Men's cultural conditioning is such that much of our self-worth comes from being able to earn and spend money and provide that money to those who depend on us. It starts with buying dinner on the first date and ends with putting money down on a mortgage for the family home. This economic validation is the hook that lures men into the provider role. In part, because it does not require learning to validate self through emotional connections that boys and men in America are traditionally not taught to create.

The more money that men generate, the more access we get to status and social standing both inside and outside the home. And the implications of this for gender conformity are huge. Why? Because the workplace is a space that typically requires a very high degree of masculine conformity. It is a narrow, constrictive box for men. And it is a box that is often mirrored by our social construction of men's roles in the home.

New York City couple and family therapist Dr. Saliha Bava notes:

> What is important is how we gender language around parenting. Many tasks done by women are called nurturing, while tasks done by men are called providing. The nuance of these language

choices clearly places the women in closer and more intimate connection to the child. It is this languaging about men that positions them as emotionally reserved in the family structure. If the man is viewed as providing and problem solving, he is valued for his activities but not his emotional connection. For many men, these activities represent their form of emotional connection. *Accordingly, we have gendered the performance of emotional connection and expression.*

Men as providers are, by definition, uninvited from the more intimate daily emotional life of the family, by virtue of our work life elsewhere (absence) and the dominant cultural definition of our role in the home. If men do not self-reflect and choose another path, we have little choice but to seek validation in our role as a provider. Which, when men's work life falters, can leave us with little or no role on which to base our identity or self-esteem. This is why unemployment is so catastrophic for men. Not only is it a huge threat economically, for many men it is also the end of our primary mode of self-validation.

Over the last twenty years, work has become increasingly elusive for millions of men. As our economy has been driven to the brink over and over by events ranging from the dot-com collapse, 9/11, the real estate bubble and the banking collapse of 2008, solid middle-class jobs have fled overseas, leaving men increasingly challenged to function as single or even dual heads of households.

Even as women have moved into the workplace, the middle-class employment opportunities for men have declined. The result is both a huge challenge for men and a huge opportunity. Because, although the devil's bargain of the Man Box may have, at one time, granted economic power to men, it continues to come with a terrible price of isolating and punishing conformity. In the Man Box, men live lives that are often deeply self-alienating.

The good news? The power of the Man Box to force rigid

conformity on men is breaking down. For better or worse, many men are no longer forced to present a rigidly normative front in the workplace or at home. And energies that were once used to present a rigid working identity can now be used to pursue innovative and adaptive ways to earn and live. This is where vast new opportunities for emotional expression and connection are emerging, especially when men move closer to the daily emotional life of the home. By participating in more of the small daily moments with our children, men are finding the vibrant emotional connection that has traditionally been denied them.

The end result? The self-reflection and cultural deconstruction that the women's movement helped normalize is now taking place in the lives of men at an accelerating rate. When men confront the Man Box by expressing gender differently, choosing to be full-time parents, seeking job satisfaction over compensation, expressing their emotions as sadness, grief or fear, long-hidden internalized narratives rise up to suppress their exploration of change. And it is in these moments that the expanding global conversation about men can give men courage to press on.

But we must all be conscious of the power of our archaic internal dialogues; of how they weave themselves through our public discourses and our unspoken expectations of each other. Good provider? Think it over.

What are you doing to a man when you call him a good provider? Are you normalizing and reinforcing the Man Box paradigm of a man who sacrifices his emotional expression and hidden aspirations to ensure a steady stream of revenue for his family? Are you relegating him to some space outside the daily emotional sphere of the family and, by extension, depriving the family of crucial male emotional modeling and connection? The image of armies of suited workingmen, marching in lockstep toward the corner office and the company car is not so far from the truth, even now. But millions of men simply no longer aspire to that. They want fuller, richer emotional lives. Lives that key on something other than the cold narrative of provider.

Ask yourself. What are the men in our lives expected to provide?

Clarity and confidence <----> Emotional openness
Singular, clear direction <----> Wide-ranging exploration
Spiritual leadership <----> Religious inquiry
Economic power <----> Economic interdependence
Gender clarity <----> Gender exploration
Assertiveness <----> Negotiation
Dominance <----> Cooperation
Providing <----> Nurturing

On Fathers' Rights

In my article for *The New York Times* titled "Fathers' Rights Needn't Hurt Women's Rights," I made the case that if a divorce must take place, fully-engaged divorced parents working in partnership to co-parent their kids is the best possible outcome for their children's emotional well-being. Although our marriages may fail, our families needn't fail as well.

We can choose to show our children that their families have not ended, just changed, and that truth will be central to their sense of security and safety. A central part of encouraging vital co-parenting agreements includes giving men equal legal rights to remain engaged parents.

What is troubling, however, is how quickly any discussion of fathers' rights or presumption of shared custody shifts to the issue of domestic violence.

The *Times* also ran an article by Kelly Behre titled, "The Fathers' Rights Movement Undermines Victims of Domestic Violence."

Behre states:

Even the more moderate groups within the fathers' rights movement engage in a backlash against feminism when they attempt to discredit the experiences of female victims of intimate partner violence ...

Let me just note here that anyone who attempts to discredit the experiences of female victims of intimate partner violence is in no way a moderate voice in the fathers' rights movement.

During a follow-up discussion titled "The Men's Rights Movement" on The Stream at Al Jazeera America (http://america.aljazeera.com/watch/shows/the-stream/articles/2014/6/19/the-men-s-rightsmovement.html), the question was asked, "Should equal custody be the baseline for divorce law and family courts in America?" Again, it was suggested that this was problematic, especially in cases of abuse.

But domestic abuse is by no means being committed only by men. The Center for Disease Control's 2010 National Intimate Partner and Sexual Violence Survey states, on page 2:

> More than 1 in 3 women (35.6%) and more than 1 in 4 men (28.5%) in the United States have experienced rape, physical violence, and/or stalking by an intimate partner in their lifetime.

To imply that domestic abuse is only inflicted against women by men is at best, ill informed, and at worst, intentionally deceptive. To acknowledge domestic violence against men does not diminish the injustices suffered by women. In fact, it gives men and women common cause to go forward together.

Violence against women is a human rights tragedy throughout the world. I will be the first to assert that women overwhelmingly bear the brunt of violence, inflicted by abusive men.

But in the sphere of intimate relationships in the U.S., the numbers become much less skewed (35.6% for women, 28.5% for men). Even if the numbers of men are somehow inflated in this study, it is clear that women also physically abuse men in significant numbers.

Any abuser, regardless of gender, forfeits his or her right to any assumption of custody. That said, we must move beyond worst-case scenarios when we talk about family law and divorce.

My son is with me three to four days a week. I am responsible for getting him to school and picking him up. I do his laundry. I pack his lunch. We do his homework together. I read to him as he falls off to sleep. We have a loving and deeply rewarding relationship and I have fought hard to ensure that he remains in my life on an almost daily basis.

His mother and I equally share the work of raising him. She is a wonderful mother. Her role in his life is central to who he is. But I am a wonderful mother, too. There is not a single task typically gendered as "woman's work" that I do not do. Sometimes when my son comes back to me from his mother's house, he will call me mother a few times. I smile when this happens. For me, this is not an error, it is an affirmation.

But I will also say this. I stay firmly in my son's life because I know that financial support is only one part of what will allow him to thrive. Our son's close relationships with both his birth parents – the valuation of which the court system has neither the capacity nor the expertise to quantify – are central to his development and well-being. Generationally, seeing his father as a caretaker as well as a wage earner will shift my son's view of what men are and how they can choose to express emotion, connection and purpose.

In my case, the payment of child support is an obligation I must fulfill. I am willing to do so because I understand that my son's life experience is directly informed by that financial support. My reliable child support payments impact everything from my relationship with his mother to the access my son has to events and activities.

It's important to note, however, that if the court believes my son's child support, as calculated, covers all his costs, it does not. None of what was allocated to my son's care by the court is spent when my son is with me. I provide those funds additionally. And because I have chosen to focus on raising my son, my income level is, in turn, reduced. It is a trade-off many co-parenting dads confront. Engaged dads are expected to provide financial support to a former spouse's parenting while their own daily parenting work is financially invisible in the eyes of the court.

In a time when more and more dads are not only paying child support but also are co-parenting, the issue of who spends that child support should be reexamined. Yes, we need laws that address the issue of fathers who do not fulfill their obligations to their children. But our legal system also needs to empower fully engaged co-parenting dads and moms as equal partners in raising their kids. These parents should be equally paying into and receiving a fair share of designated child support funds and other rights based on what they are committed to do in support of their kids and their new post-divorce families.

We must create new standards, culturally and legally, for the deeply humane and collaborative child raising solutions that are evolving all around us, or risk killing the very change we are seeking to create for men and women alike.

Boys, Independence and Touch Isolation

It is a mandate of American culture that we teach boys to be independent even as we encourage girls to touch, share and connect.

The traditional narrative is as follows: Girls talk. Boys win. Girls are provided for. Boys provide for them. Girls love. Boys win love. Sometime around kindergarten age, boys are expected to be strong enough to begin soothing their own wounds and winning their own battles in the world. Perhaps this shift takes place when they are six years old, perhaps when they are eight; but American boys are typically expected to self-soothe, stand on their own two feet and "shake it off," because otherwise they might end up weak. And weakness in boys is the night terror of American parents.

More than anything else, American parents fear a son who clings; a son who is needy. Somewhere out there lurks a fat, confused, unmotivated lump of a man who is parked weeping on the basement couch at age thirty. It is the American parenting nightmare.

And so, we start early with our sons, privileging self-reliance and emotional toughness over the encouragement of close physical contact and emotional expression. We gently but firmly wean them off hugs, kisses and talking about their emotions. We subject them to this uniquely American touch isolation because we don't want them to be momma's boys. We don't want them to be crybabies. We hesitate to reach out and hold them when they cry. We hesitate to talk about their sadness or their fears. We push them out into the world, in part to avoid the messy business of helping them navigate emotional complexity. Love me, son but do it *over there*. Love me from first base. Love me from the front of the class. Love me from the trading floor. Love me from Iraq.

And the saddest part of this entire equation is the following fact: The ability to be cared for and comforted is a crucial human capacity, without which we cannot live fully connected, emotionally intimate lives.

Poor American parents, we've got the definition of strength all wrong. We're so busy ensuring independence in our little sons that we are giving birth to generation after generation of men who can't create community. Who lack empathy and the ability to engage and appreciate difference. Who withdraw into isolated emotional bunkers from which to stand their ground.

It is this cult of independence that has created generations of alpha obsessed, my-way-or-the-highway men, privileging financial Darwinism and conspicuous consumption over every other metric. There is no safety net. Nor should there be.

This is all taking place on a vast scale, which ultimately is laying economic waste to our disconnected, gated communities; and ironically enough, casting baby boomer parents into the Dickensian drudgery of Walmart greeters; eventually warehousing dear old mom and dad in bleak retirement homes, starved for the very human contact they denied their own sons. A real estate bubble here. A shock and awe there. The American cult of independence has unleashed cultural Armageddon against us all while holding itself accountable to no one.

Need proof? Look no further than the Wall Street banks and Enrons of the world. It's dog eats dog. No more, no less.

The cult of independence tells little boys over and over again to "man up" as if that is the single answer to all the world's problems. And, not surprisingly, we are dealing with a lot of angry, bullying boys, who, as an expression of their emotional isolation, lash out over and over again. Man up, indeed.

Bullying is not some simple extension of male energy. It is not biologically inevitable. But when emotional toughness is our society's highest valued personal trait, bullying is inevitable, because bullying is, at its base, an expression of loss, isolation, grief and jealousy. It is the rage of boys who are wracked with confusion. "What is suddenly wrong with wanting to be held, comforted and kept safe? *Yesterday you held me. Today you pushed me away.*"

The echo of this litany plays out over and over in the collapse of our adult relationships. "Yesterday you held me, today you pushed me away." The stress cracks and fractures of male rejection and insecurity run deep in our society. The voices of male anger rant across the internet; the voices of men expressing anger at women. Women who don't connect. Women who are aloof and unkind. Women who simply aren't there at all.

These are the voices of men who have bottled up so much pain that self-reflection is seemingly impossible. You might as well stare into the sun. And so, they blame everyone else. These men are unable to see their own pain in others, because no one saw it in them. They are unable to connect emotionally after a lifetime of conditioning to adopt tough alpha male stoicism over emotional connection.

And women are as responsible as men for privileging and perpetuating the American cult of independence. Treading the cartoon catwalks of gender even as they wax disappointed in the very male stoicism they are a party to perpetuating.

American women talk a good game about wanting men to connect emotionally, but it takes a strong woman to care for a man in the same way that men are asked to care for women. When the tears and insecurity of men are finally teased out, many women say, "You're not the man I thought I was with. You're just looking for your mommy."

Indeed, some of us are. But the shock of that dirty little secret is only a challenge if you expect your man to provide emotional care for you without seeking it in return. Because when you open up the well of suppressed male pain, it's a storm that will wreck every convenient macho Hollywood assumption about men we ever had.

We are not strong because we have not faced our own demons. In part, because when men attempt to do so publicly, we are shamed and rejected, often by our own wives and partners. Immediately. Made to walk the plank of emotional rejection all over again.

Over and over men tell me that this is the baseline message they get about sharing their emotions. "Show me what you're feeling, but don't show me more than I'm comfortable with."

To express emotion, display grief, show vulnerability and process pain requires a degree of personal strength and self-reliance that far outstrips what is needed to bully or dominate others.

The capacity to be vulnerable in American culture is nothing short of superhuman. It's the first step toward self-reflection. And we Americans don't do self-reflection. Because it smacks of self-doubt. And real men always know what they think. They always know what to do. They never doubt themselves. Ever.

Never mind the fact that self-reflection is a key to finding true contentment in our lives. The prohibition against self-reflection means that men (and women) bottle up self-doubt and pain, creating a wellspring of anger that makes them defend their point of view like it is God's own truth.

We are a nation of bullies, because that's what bullies are – people who have avoided self-reflection for so long that to do so now would be like unleashing a bomb inside themselves. Better to keep a lid on it all. Better to attack anyone who says otherwise.

In America? Bullies are running the show. The wounded, angry little boys are at the wheel and they are weakest of us all.

The strategies men use to try and hide our pain are doing generational damage over and over again. Men, isolated from connection by our emotion-phobic American culture, seek to satisfy a lifetime of need for connection through their romantic partners, a burden which few women (or men), no matter how loving, could realistically be expected to fulfill.

This is the reason that frequency of sex often becomes the single most challenging issue for couples. Men often key on sex as an attempt to bridge our way back to the gentle comforting touch of our distant childhoods that, long absent, can never quite be recaptured or recalled. The orgasm becomes a surrogate for that lost contact, a moment of male safety and security when the white flare of pleasure leaves loss behind. For ten seconds we know peace. Maybe twenty. But like we handle everything else with a potential emotional component in our lives, we American men are terribly prone to approaching sex mechanically, staring inward at our own flaring confusion instead of looking outward into the mysterious miracle of our partners.

In that moment, sex becomes another exercise in internalizing our experiences instead of surrendering to the interdependence, which we have never learned to engage. And surprise – in relationship after relationship, romance withers. Sex falls off. But we men continue to go to the well of cold, mechanical sex, long after our lovers have lost their passion for it, because like everything else in our emotional landscapes, we have confused the ghost of contact with really living our lives.

Meanwhile, men and women alike are absorbing the generational impact of contentious and angry divorce, shattered relationships and the ongoing war between the sexes, which is typically informed by angry binary dialogues about sex, sex and sex.

Men heckle women about frequency of sex because we key on it as our only authentic moments of contact in lives otherwise starved of connection. Sex becomes the only moment men mark as being truly cared for emotionally. Sex speaks to the wounded little boy and his endless appetite for me, me, me. And drowned out by our relentless emphasis on sex, every other gesture of caring in all the other parts of our relationships are not marked. Are not valued. Instead, the only marker of a good relationship is frequency of sex. Which, because we avoid emotional intimacy, is fueled by the cartoon daydreams of porn instead of the deeper resonance of love.

And regardless of what mirroring issues women have in our culture, until men stop self-medicating through a repetitive and mechanical reliance on sexual orgasm, we will never be in a position to demand equal emotional accountability from women. As long as sex remains the proof of our connection and validity, we will always be at risk of reducing our human relationships to that narcotic standard.

It ain't a pretty picture. And men and women share in what has been created.

When you raise boys and cut them off from comforting touch and connection, you sever their connection to the security they need to develop emotionally. This is what is behind the attachment parenting movement. This is why consistent physical contact, hugs and touch, are so central to the healthy development of young children. And this is why we have to make space for physical and emotional connection with our boys in the same way we do with our daughters, because the fallout of failing to do so can be catastrophic.

When I was six years old, my parents were in the throes of an impending marital collapse. During that time, they withdrew from my brother and me. I can only guess this was due to depression and emotional turmoil.

My brother was a year and a half older than I. He had always picked on me some, but when my father left our lives he became an animal. He bullied me through extremely close physical contact.

Not so much punching, although there was some of that; it was more about breaking down my autonomy. About getting inside my boundaries and proving he could do it whenever he wanted. Early each morning, he would get up and force me out of my bed. Then he would get in it, saying, "This is my bed now." Standing there shivering, I had no choice but to get in his bed. I recall how his bed stank of him. His smell is what remains with me to this day.

He would pin me down and dribble long gobs of spit in my face. He would bend my arm behind my back until I submitted to whatever he wanted. He was always a ticking, angry time bomb. Always ready to go off and do something. An unending threat that my mother and stepfather seemed unable or unwilling to curtail. My mother's solution was to tell us over and over again to "work it out." How do you work out being attacked?

I can smell him now, forty years later, as I sit here typing. What he did has made an imprint on me that I cannot shake. And although I have not spoken with him in decades, I need not look very far inside myself to find him there. I can still feel his anger. His rage. His breath on the side of my face. His presence was always too close, too oppressive, and too sensory. My arrival must have deprived him of something central in his young life. I'm guessing access to and contact with our mother. Whatever it was, he was my personal bully and he remained so, until I left the house for good.

I think I understand my brother even as I remain haunted by the terrible luck of the draw that condemned me to grow up with him. He is a huge symbol of loss. He deprived me of something I needed terribly. A big brother I could count on. A male role model I could aspire to. That, coupled with the absence of my father, left me with no model for what it means to be a good man, or for that matter, a man at all. But I still understand my brother. He and I both needed comfort and connection, connection that was stripped out of our lives. Perhaps his physicality with me was his way of getting the human touch he needed. But it was filtered through rage.

My brother needed connection.

Connection that we strip out of our young boys' lives for far less valid reasons. Because we think they need to be tougher. Because we think independence is a core American value and a viable central philosophy for creating a good life. It is not. Independence is the illusion of strength.

Our cultural obsession with independence is fracturing our society because it teaches us that we don't need each other when, in fact, we do. We are, in fact, hardwired to be *inter*dependent. We need each other emotionally, physically and spiritually, and the vast majority of men and women are starving for interdependent connection in our lives.

There will always be men who are comfortable with what might be called traditional masculinity. Good for you guys. If that works for you, go with it. But we need to ensure there is a much wider cultural space for men who want to perform masculinity differently.

We have to break out of what many people are calling the Man Box. And as part of breaking out, we need to stop privileging independence over *inter*dependence. We need to connect in the full range of ways that make sense for us. And, equally importantly, we need to find partners in our lives who will do the same. To any man or woman out there, if your partner seeks to suppress your emotions and discourages your self-reflection, dump them, because they're poison, plain and simple.

In its most positive sense, freedom isn't located in the capacity to function without reliance on others. True freedom comes from being socially literate and culturally fluent, giving us the ability to engage the widest possible range of communities, contexts and interpersonal options.

True freedom comes from being fully engaged and connected in the world, so we can choose our path, not based on what we fear as unfamiliar, but based instead on what we know from a wide range of diverse experience is right for us. When we live in a web of interconnection, we are no longer at risk for being cast out, economically lost, or spiritually isolated. The human web is too vast. There are always places we can shift to and seek options. The wider the range of connectivity we have in our lives, the wider the range of options for dealing with adversity. This alleviates fear and provides security.

At the heart of connection is our willingness and capacity to hold and care for each other. This is a central life lesson we can simultaneously learn from and teach our young sons, by keeping them close instead of pushing them away. Then we will create a generation of boys who can connect physically and emotionally, which will help heal the world for us all.

Thinking About Experimenting with Gender? Don't

Recently, an editor at The Good Men Project whose opinions I highly respect made a comment during a discussion on gender: "Men can legally express gender in any way they like." As if that particular battle has been won and now it's simply up to men to throw off the chains of our own fears and express gender in more diverse ways. The path is clear.

From a legal standpoint this is probably true. Our society is saturated with enough examples of men going against gender stereotypes that we now, in terms of case law and social norms, fully expect that some small percentage of men will express themselves in outrageous, gender-bending ways.

At the extreme edge of gender expression, drag queens like RuPaul are creating the most subversive kind of gender theater, poking fun at glamour, sexuality, power and our culture's brutally restrictive self-image. But most drag queens have no doubt paid a high price for their expressions of gender. They likely have been forced to put distance between themselves and members of their family, been cut off from the communities they grew up in and most likely, live in fear of being attacked economically, socially or physically for their choices, especially if they continue to blend their gender performances into their daily lives.

High camp drag is such a potent expression of gender theater that it leaves a massive space between itself and the daily expression of gender as performed by most men. Although it creates space for more diverse expressions of gender, it is not a threat to the oppressive gender conformity that society imposes on the vast majority of men.

In fact, the drag show caricature may well serve to enforce gender conformity as it so clearly defines the choice between "us" and "them" that men are confronted with when they think about their own secret desires for change, however humble. Because, legalities aside, if you want to remain a member of the "us" group, you had better think long and hard about what that membership requires of you.

When your male boss says a passing female co-worker is hot, it may adversely impact your child's college fund to say anything other than "Hell, yeah." Sure, your boss is an idiot, but everybody knows that right?

It's in economically driven spaces that the most lowbrow expressions of gender conformity are enforced and adopted to the detriment of all. Because people make the most blunt and general conceptual alliances when they perceive their economic interests to be at stake, often overcompensating in ways that damage their internal sense of personal integrity.

Sadly, the most oppressive gender-conformity-enforcing economic spaces do not exist where money is earned. They exist where it is spent. For many men who are seeking to express their gender in more diverse ways, the most potent adversary to change can end up being their own wives and families.

Men in Western culture are living with the fallout of generations of female economic disempowerment. Even as it has become culturally normative for women to be accepted as CEOs of major corporations, as attorneys, doctors, professors and more, the narrative of man as breadwinner remains firmly entrenched in our culture, due in part to payment disparities that still linger here.

While the pace of economic progress for women in Western culture is dramatic, the narratives of female economic disempowerment are slow to shift, ultimately taking perhaps a generation or more to change. This is in part because it remains a legitimate issue and in part because women are loath to give up the leverage this narrative creates in political, social, personal, and, of course, legal contexts.

Put simply, liberated views of gender and manhood are all fun and games until a baby shows up. Then the gender roles men are expected to fulfill can suddenly become far more draconian and rigid. It's as if the 20-year economic timeline that a baby represents creates a panic in which cultural complexity, uncertainty and risk-taking are dismissed as dangerous indulgences that must be put aside for the good of the family.

Suddenly, people inside and outside the family want to know that the man is going to conform and provide. The role of being a good dad and a good breadwinner dials down to a simple equation: conformity equals security. In these moments, men sign up for a lifetime of gender conformity, setting in place patterns of behavior and unspoken relational agreements that may never be undone.

Recently, a 7-year-old boy I know, a friend of my son, disclosed his interest in the "My Little Pony" show, a program clearly designed for and marketed to girls. When I asked him if his friends at school liked the show, he shook his head gravely. "I would never tell them I like the show. Never," was his response. At seven, he is quite clear about which parts of him should remain hidden.

And the lessons for boys and men on how to be normative never stop coming. They inform our littlest daily decisions right through to the biggest decisions of our lives. As a man, I know for a fact that wearing bright colors is considered a bit "out there." It's a gutsy move. It might seem ... odd. What if I roll up my khakis? Or wear pink socks? God forbid I don a sparkly hair beret before heading into a client meeting.

I know for a fact how to walk in a way that will blend in. I know how to talk. I know how to carry my backpack. How to hold my son's hand. It's all clearly prescribed. *The man's handbook, unwritten and known by all.* And that's just the little stuff.

What if a man wants to express his sexuality in more gender fluid ways?

When a man tries to take some of his more private expressions of gender public, his own spouse can become the cop who bars the door. Why? Because the economic and social implications of not being viewed as normative, especially gender normative, can be terribly frightening. When men seek to make the private more public, the fears of being rejected socially or professionally causes a lot of unspoken agreements about priorities to kick in.

It is in this space between the private and the public where our courage to make change around gender often fails us. This is where irreversible damage gets done to men and women equally, as economic and social fears force gender conformity in soul-killing ways. And although men may be legally allowed to express gender in any way they see fit, the circumstances in which they find themselves can often lead to a rush to frame themselves as normative, seeking the security of being marked as normal when legal or financial goals hang in the balance.

At which point, the tragedy of modern post-industrial life so predictably unfolds. As men and women buy into the necessity of suppressing their non-normative sides, the very parts of them that make them vibrant and distinctive individuals, they willingly immerse themselves in a vacuous culture of interpersonal isolation; a twilight world of disconnection. In an effort to create security, they commit to living in self-imposed communities of homogeneous alienation and create isolating family structures that ultimately fail and collapse.

For men, economic security and the workplace conformity it typically demands can lead to the suppression of their most diverse emotional aspects. The resulting suppression of these vibrant internal dialogues contributes to the epidemic levels of depression, drug abuse, violence and suicide among men. The result is men living lives of quiet, isolated desperation, mirrored by wives who in turn are trapped in equally narrow and self-defeating gender roles. It is a devil's bargain struck from fear and economic uncertainty; the by-product of a culture that teaches us to value materialism and financial security as paramount markers of success.

Make no mistake. Worldwide, women are suffering under economic systems that make them nothing less than indentured slaves to their husbands and families; subject to rape, violence and murder on a scale that few men in our comparatively pampered Western culture are even willing to acknowledge. NPR aired a harrowing report on the more than one hundred sexual assaults against women that took place in Tahrir Square during the recent pro-democracy protests in Egypt. Take a moment to listen to it. It will leave you shocked and outraged. It is much worse than my simple summary here suggests. Moreover, hundreds of millions of men and women worldwide are subject to lives so difficult that the relative challenges of emotional isolation and martini materialism in Western culture are nothing less than laughable by comparison.

But if we are to move forward in creating a world devoid of oppression and systemic abuse, we cannot dismiss the leading edges of change as being nothing more than bourgeois anxiety, unworthy of being addressed against the greater backdrop of global sexism and racism.

We must acknowledge and nurture the evolution of our own cultural thinking if we are to create systems that do not simply sustain oppression of the weakest by the strongest. Part of this change will come by tearing down the false, narrow and ultimately tedious standards of a normative masculinity. A task that only the luckiest and wealthiest of us on the leading edge of global prosperity are at liberty to even consider addressing.

It is a task that will require significant long-term emotional courage from both men and women; a willingness to live with change and uncertainty as we relearn who we are in relationships to each other. It will require that women encourage their men and themselves to live more fully expressive lives, even if that opens the door to changes neither can predict. But whatever the costs we confront in challenging our deep-seated fears of being deemed non-normative, the results will be more fully realized and satisfying lives for ourselves, our children and our communities.

Here are a few questions worth pondering:

• Is there a correlation between the continuing role of men as primary breadwinners and their relatively uniform public expression of gender?

• Are women more fearful of being socially rejected then men? How does this impact the way they construct their family's public persona?

• Are gay men freer to pursue a more liberated expression of gender because they are not in partnership with women?

• Why are feminine-presenting straight men invisible in our culture while feminine-presenting gay men are quite prominent?

• How do we view the intersection of gender diversity and parenting for men? How do men need to present in order to seem like good parents?

• What action can we take collectively to signal we are open to gender diversity among men, especially straight men?

Boys and the Burden of Shame

In America, shame is how we make people do what we want. We shame our children to get them to attend to us. We use shame as a heavy-handed shortcut in our adult relationships. We use it in our political debates and public discourses. Whether it's about the cultural, the sexual, the political, or the religious, we don't just disagree, we shame those who don't speak or behave in ways we approve of. We express shock, anger and outrage at their core personhood. We say, "You should be ashamed of yourself."

This is not a right-wing or left-wing issue. This is not about class, race or gender. This issue cuts across all segments of American society. Shaming in our American culture is epidemic.

We don't just tell our children about right and wrong, we go a step further with statements like, "Don't be so selfish" or "You are exhausting" or worse, "You have disappointed me, failed me."

We shame our kids into behaving, which may be effective in the short term, but do we really understand what we are training them into? When we shame our kids, two things are happening: we are training them to feel bad about themselves, and we are encouraging them to shame others.

Physical punishment is tied directly to the epidemic of shaming in America. The Child Trends DataBank reports that in 2012 a nationally representative survey showed 77 percent of men and 65 percent of women 18 to 65 years old agreed that a child sometimes needs a "good hard spanking."

Child Trends notes:

Use of corporal punishment is linked to negative outcomes for children (e.g., delinquency, antisocial behavior, psychological problems, and alcohol and drug abuse), and may be indicative of ineffective parenting. Research also finds that the number of problem behaviors observed in adolescence is related to the amount of spanking a child receives. The greater the age of the child, the stronger the relationship.

This is why parenting advocates ask us to forego spanking. They also ask us to point out the errors, or poor decisions our kids make without slipping into condemning the children themselves. This crucial distinction is central if we are to break the cycle of shame in our culture.

This summer, my wife and I were swimming in the Frio River in Texas. It was a beautiful sunny day. There were a hundred or more people hanging out on the river.

In front of us towered a thirty-foot high slab of rock jutting vertically out of the water. Kids were using a rope line tied at the top to scale the steep incline of the slab and jump off the other side into a deep, blue swimming hole. One boy had climbed to the top but could not bring himself to jump. Each time he tried to jump, he would start toward the edge, involuntarily sit down and then scoot back up towards the top the rock. He tried over and over again, but he could not jump off. Kids were lining up behind him, going past him, and jumping.

His father began to call out to him from below, encouraging him to be brave and jump. His dad was supportive, but his voice carried all across the river. More and more people began watching as the boy would take a few halting steps toward the edge and then panic and back up. His fear became a public spectacle. Climbing back down the way he came was also a frightening prospect; the sheer face of the rock where the rope dangled would have been very difficult to descend. Jumping was likely the safer option.

After about five minutes of this, a single boy below in the water yelled out. His voice, high pitched and clear as a bell, rose and echoed off the cliffs around us.

"What are you, a girl? You're just a scared girl!"

The shaming moment had arrived, held in check thus far, by the number of adults interspersed among the kids in the river. The boy above was deeply ashamed of himself for not being able to master his fear; we could all see it in his face. But now he was like a hunted animal, caught between his fear of getting injured and his fear of being publicly humiliated. His dad began to climb the rock face to get to him.

Another man from the boy's family group began to call to him from below. "Just jump! Just count to three and jump!" There was a tone of impatience in his voice. Was he, in some way, feeling shame at the boy's fear? Or was the man genuinely concerned about the emotional impact the boy would face as the seconds dragged on?

The people below watched the increasingly painful public spectacle. When the boy in the water called the boy on the rock "a girl," I was immediately aware of how many girls were also watching and listening. Perhaps a few of the girls on the bank smiled at the ruthless efficiency of this taunt. I don't recall. But the dozen or so mothers, faces upturned, were not laughing.

In moments like this, shame moves in ripples through a population in different ways, depending on one's age or view of the world. Clearly, someone had regularly shamed the boy in the water. Was it his parents, his teachers, or kids at school? Who knows? But the boy had learned how powerful a tool shame is, and he now casually employed it in a very public way against another boy who was in distress. He not only shamed the boy on the rock, he degraded every girl within hearing and left every adult in the area with a choice: Do I remain silent or call out something supportive, or what?

We began yelling encouragement to the kid, but it seemed to only make him more aware of how public this humiliation had become.

The boy's father made it to the top of the rock and took his son's hand. They got ready to jump together, hand in hand, and then the boy balked. He was still too afraid. His father decided that dragging his son over the side by the hand was too risky. He shifted his strategy, picked up his son; spoke to him quietly, and then tossed him off. As the boy fell, he pitched forward into a belly flop. Arms flailing, his body made that hollow pop sound when he hit the water; blinding pain to go with the humiliation.

The boy's father jumped right behind him. The boy lunged up out of the water yelling, "Oh my god!" over and over, gasping for air and weeping. It was a train-crash-horrible moment. Slowly, everyone went back to his or her conversations. The father took his son aside and sat with him as he cried it out. I looked away, trying to give them some kind of privacy there on the muddy riverbank.

What keeps coming back to me is how shame was operating all around us that day.

To begin with, the boy in the water, the boy who taunted the kid on the rock, was clearly taking pleasure in employing shame. It was a glory moment for him. You could see him looking excited and proud as he taunted the other boy, glancing around in the moment, looking for acknowledgement. The implication was, "I'm only saying what everyone else is thinking, right?" It was as if he expected others to acknowledge his shaming as an act of leadership.

For many boys and girls, shaming is a central tool for climbing higher in the pecking order, accruing authority, and declaring their conformity. This boy learned it; now he was using it. How much shame of his own he was burdened with I don't know. But it is safe to say that the fiercest advocates for employing shame are, themselves, often victims of it.

I was acutely aware of how familiar this all felt to me, and probably to other adults who were watching. When I was a boy, witnessing some kid being publicly shamed was so commonplace as to be a daily or even hourly occurrence. Shame was the language we all spoke; the cruel machinery of the all-important pecking order.

This scene brought back the nausea I had always felt watching victims (usually other boys) being force-fed their own self-loathing. It might be about their bodies, or their clothes, or their lack of a girlfriend. It was always something they had little power over; always something ultimately unfair or vacuously irrelevant, which just made it all the more humiliating. The trick was not to be the target of a public shaming. Never be the target.

Meanwhile, the boy on the rock; what about him? When I saw how quickly his struggle to jump collapsed into public shame, I knew he also had been shamed, maybe not by his father, but perhaps his peers? I could see shame radiating off him, as he stood suspended between his fear of getting injured and his fear of failure. Failing at what? Jumping off a rock? What made this moment so powerful a trap for him?

He did not have the confidence, the self-esteem, to simply say, "Nope, no thanks. This is not for me." So, he dangled, frozen, in a display of crippling, public shame.

I'm also left wondering, did he automatically assume our contempt as he scanned our upturned faces? Sadly, the answer is probably yes. Because once we have been trained to be ashamed of ourselves, we don't need active confirmation from others. We supply it on their behalf. We assume others are disappointed in us, even those we love. We fill in the blanks between others and us with the most damaging possible messages, even when those messages are not their intention at all.

It is this willingness, this *need* to fill the blanks with self-condemnation and shame that collapses relationships and destroys marriages. It leads to all manner of self-destructive behaviors. Shame fuels itself, becomes its own self-fulfilling prophecy. And no one, no matter how kind or supportive they are in a relationship, can successfully love someone who has succumbed to the voice of shame.

If I was that boy's dad (and I think his dad did a good job under difficult circumstances) I might have made a different choice. I would have said, first and foremost, "You don't have to do this. Period. We'll get you down. Just back off and sit."

But the boy felt he had to jump off the rock. Once he faltered, shame rushed in immediately. By not jumping, he felt he had failed his friends and his family. The messages this boy supplied himself, the ease with which he delivered the most brutal self-assessment possible, left him no room for alternative courses of action. This is when shame is most destructive.

It strips us of our natural sense of self-preservation and replaces it with a willingness to do anything to get off the arbitrary and hateful hot seat as defined by whatever bully might seek to shame us.

For adults, shame can be about anything and everything: our sexual selves, our interpersonal failings, our imperfect bodies, our difficult pasts, our losses, the relentless litany of our regrets. Shame can leach the joy out of life. It is a loop of self-destructive internal dialogues that blind us to what is good and magical and strong in us. Shame is a sure-fire recipe for depression, alcoholism, drug abuse, divorce, alienation and despair.

And because we Americans are so prone to using shame to get our way with others, it has infused our public and private lives. It is so universal that we simply cannot grasp the vastness of it. It is the forest we cannot see for the trees. It is the very air we breathe and the water we drink. Shame is everywhere, insinuating itself into the memories of our childhoods and the voices of our loved ones. And the only clue we have of how universal shame actually is, is the privileged position it holds as that little voice in our heads that whispers over and over, "You're never going to be good enough."

Can we overcome shame in our daily lives? The answer is yes. And here's how.

Dr. Saliha Bava, a couple and family therapist with a practice in New York City, has a simple and powerful answer for dealing with the culture of shame – *talk about it*:

Shame thrives on confusion and misunderstanding. When you illuminate shame by talking about it, its power diminishes. When we talk about shame, as shame, we can share how we intend to be heard, because so often, others can hear statements as shaming that are not intended that way.

Shame is also deeply personal. We cannot know what others might view as shaming unless we talk with them about it. And this includes our friends, wives, husbands, parents and children.

When we talk openly about the culture of shame, the activity of talking shifts the culture. In the moment we speak, we change our path forward. Change our lives. We have the power to replace the culture of shame with something new that is getting created. What I choose to create is called the culture of permission. You may want to choose something different. Perhaps, for you, it is a culture of compassion, or a culture of discovery.

As couples and families, we can create these conversational spaces in which we talk with curiosity about what shame is for us as individuals. We can create spaces for listening. Create spaces for difference.

These are meant to be ongoing conversations that weave in and out of our daily talk. As part of this, we can help ourselves and the children in our lives identify moments of shaming. We can learn to spot shame when it appears. Once we see shame for what it is, we can identify it throughout our lives and guard against letting it have a hold on us.

Dr. Bava's point is clear. If we don't talk about the messages we give and get, and clarify our intentions for others, the culture of shame will, by default, define those messages for us.

So, let's start pushing back against the culture of shame by bringing it out of the shadows and into the light. Let's make the choice to talk about shame, and let's start by talking with the people we love most.

Men, Homophobia and Touch

Boys imitate what they see. If what they see is emotional distance, guardedness, and coldness between men, they will grow up to imitate that behavior. ... What do boys learn when they do not see men with close friendships, where there are no visible models of intimacy in a man's life beyond his spouse?
– Kindlon and Thompson, *Raising Cain* (With thanks to Brett & Kate McKay)

Recently, I wrote an article titled "The Lack of Gentle Platonic Touch in Men's Lives is a Killer" in which I asked people to consider the following:

American men, in an attempt to avoid any possible hint of committing unwanted sexual touch, are foregoing gentle platonic touch in their lives. I call it *touch isolation*.

Homophobic social stigmas, the long-standing challenges of rampant sexual abuse, and a society steeped in a generations-old puritanical mistrust of physical pleasure have created an isolating trap in which American men can go for days or weeks at a time without touching another human being. The implications of touch isolation for men's health and happiness are huge.

Gentle platonic touch is central to the early development of infants. It continues to play an important role throughout men's and women's lives in terms of our development, health and emotional well-being, including into old age.

When I talk about gentle platonic touch, I'm not talking about a pat on the back, or a handshake, but instead contact that is lasting and meant to provide connection and comfort. Think, leaning on someone for a few minutes, holding hands, rubbing their back, or sitting close together not out of necessity but out of choice.

Yet, culturally, we suppress gentle platonic touch in men, and it starts when they are very young boys.

While babies and toddlers are held, cuddled, and encouraged to practice gentle touch during the first years of their lives, that contact often drops off for boys when they cease to be toddlers.

Young boys are encouraged to "shake it off" and "be tough" when they are hurt. Along with this get-tough narrative, boys find that their options for gentle platonic touch simply fade away. Mothers and fathers often back off from holding or cuddling their young boys. Boys who seek physical holding when hurt are stigmatized as crybabies.

By the time they are approaching puberty, many boys have learned to touch only in aggressive ways through roughhousing or team sports. And if they do seek gentle touch in their lives, it is expected to take place in the exclusive and highly sexualized context of dating. This puts massive amounts of pressure on young girls – who are unlikely to be able to shoulder the emotional burden this represents.

And worse, touch deprivation faced by young boys who are unable to find a girlfriend is overwhelming. And what about boys who are gay? In a nutshell, we expect children in their early teens to somehow undo a lifetime of touch aversion and physical isolation through dating.

The emotional impact of coming of age in our touch-averse, homophobic culture is terribly damaging. It's no wonder our young people face an epidemic of sexual abuse, unwanted pregnancy, rape, drug and alcohol abuse.

If you think men have always been hands-off with each other, have a look at an amazing collection of historic photos compiled by Brett and Kate McKay for an article they titled: "Bosom Buddies: A Photo History of Male Affection." It's a remarkable look at male camaraderie as expressed though physical touch, in photos dating back to the earliest days of photography. Spend some time looking at these remarkable images (like the one above). You'll get a visceral sense of what has been lost to men.

The McKays note in their article:

But at the turn of the 20th century ... Thinking of men as either "homosexual" or "heterosexual" became common. And this new category of identity was at the same time pathologized – decried by psychiatrists as a mental illness, by ministers as a perversion, and by politicians as something to be legislated against. As this new conception of homosexuality as a stigmatized and onerous identifier took root in American culture, men began to be much more careful to not send messages to other men, and to women, that they were gay. And this is the reason why, it is theorized, men have become less comfortable with showing affection towards each other over the last century.

In America today, if you put ten people in the room where two men are touching for a moment too long, someone will make a gay joke, express distaste, or even pick a fight. The enforcement of touch prohibition between men can be as subtle as a raised eyebrow or as punitive as a fistfight, and you never know where it will come from or how quickly it will escalate; it's just as likely to be a woman as to be a man who enforces the homophobic/touch-averse stigma.

And yet, we know that touch between men or women has been proven to be a source of comfort, connection and self-esteem. But while women are allowed much more public contact, American men are not. How we allow men to perform masculinity is highly restrictive. Charlie Glickman writes eloquently about this in his article, "Escape the 'Act Like a Man' Box" on The Good Men Project website (https://goodmenproject.com).

Male touch isolation is one of many powerful reasons why I support gay rights initiatives. The sooner being gay is completely normalized, the sooner homophobic prohibitions against touch will be taken off straight men. As much as gay men have faced the brunt of homophobic violence, straight men have been banished to a desert of physical isolation by these same homophobic fanatics who police lesbians and gays in our society. The result has been a generation of American men who do not hug each other, do not hold hands and cannot sit close together without the homophobic litmus test kicking in.

The lack of touch in men's lives results in a higher likelihood of depression, alcoholism, and mental and physical illness. Put simply, touch isolation is making men's lives less healthy and lonelier.

Recently, when visiting my 87-year-old father for a few days, I made a point to reach out and touch him more; to make contact; to express my affection, not just by flying a thousand miles for a visit, but to touch the man once I got there. It may seem simple but choosing to do so is not always a simple thing. It can give rise to a lifetime of internal voices, many of which speak of loss and missed opportunities.

I hugged him. I put my arm around him as we shared a cigar and cocktails. I touched him whenever I walked past his chair.

On evenings when we watched a movie, I would sit on the floor, take off his shoes and massage his bare feet. It is something I will remember when he is gone. Something I did right. Something that said to him, "I love you." Spoken on the same deep touch levels by which he connected with me when I was a toddler sitting next to him, his strong arm around me as I watched TV fifty years ago.

We need to empower men to touch. We need to heal our sexually repressed/obsessed American culture and put an end to distorted and hateful parts of our society that allow homophobic people to police all men everywhere down to the very tips of our fingertips.

It's too late in my life for the impact of these stigmas to be fully undone, but I have great hope for my son. When we collectively normalize gay life and relationships, my son, whatever his sexual orientation turns out to be, will be free to express platonic affection for others, be they men or women, in any way he sees fit. The rabid homophobes who have preached hate in America for far too long will finally be silenced, and men will be free to reach out and touch each other without fear of being labeled as somehow less of a man.

The Dark Side of Progressive Women

A while back, I followed a series of tweets about men and the expression of emotions. At one point, a woman who was participating said the following:

I'm having a hard time formulating all my issues here. It boggles my mind that we've been asking [men] to be more emotional and engaged, and when they become emotional and engaged we say, "That's too much!" I mean, talk about expecting perfection. Life is growth and effort.

I went to sleep thinking about a question, which can haunt men like myself: Do some women who encourage men to "be more emotional and engaged" end up losing respect for the men who do so?

Think of the moment when Lucy yanks the football out on Charlie Brown.

I admit it could take a decade or two to unpack all the implications of the phrase "be more emotional and engaged." I'm also aware of the exhausting and overworked meme of women who talk about wanting a nice guy but go for the jerks in the world. That narrative smacks far too much of either self-pity or opportunism depending on the man promoting it.

What I am talking about instead is the moment at which our deeply layered cultural conditioning collides with our social or ideological aspirations – what we think we want, versus what we discover we need.

This request by women for men to be more emotional and engaged covers a vast range of relational and functional markers. It also means very different things to different people.

I take it to mean that men are being asked to: 1) increase emotional expression in their relationships; and 2) address basic issues of fairness in how work is organized and done in any partnership, up to and including marriage.

If the stereotypical 1970s dad brought home the paycheck and did little to help raise the kids or clean the house, the modern man is asked to be much more engaged. In some cases, he may be asked to take over the home and the primary childcare while his wife pursues a higher-paying career.

This cultural trend may be ideologically driven, a function of the breakdown of gender silos, or the result of simple economic necessity. Regardless of the source, the trend is out there.

So, if I ended my day thinking about the tweets I read, I ran smack into the other bookend the next morning – a book review by Liz Mundy of the *San Francisco Chronicle*. She is reviewing a novel by British author Rachel Cusk, titled *Aftermath: On Marriage and Separation*.

Mundy writes:

Not long ago, in an online blog of *The Wall Street Journal*, a wife made a confession. A high-earning editor and the breadwinner in her family, she admitted that she resents her husband for being supportive and domestically hands-on. Far from being grateful that he makes her job and family life possible by taking on the role of primary caregiver to their son, she feels burdened and jealous. While some of her objections are fair – supporting a household is scary, as men have long known – others, she acknowledged, aren't.

Her piece is a reminder that women, like men, can be emotionally retrograde even as they are progressive and ambitious; it's not always men who have trouble adapting to female achievement and female earning.

The same dynamic is at work in *Aftermath*, Rachel Cusk's bleak and rather bravely unsympathetic memoir of marital dissolution.

Cusk sketches a scenario whereby she maneuvered her husband into the role of househusband, then scorned him for occupying it. She is not sure whom to blame for this radical inconsistency: her feminism, her parents, her schooling, or simply whatever was in the water when she was growing up.

It got me thinking; maybe this whole gender equality thing is a hell of a lot harder than we know, because it's not just about men and women taking on new roles and ways of being, it's about unpacking the very real and disruptive conditioning the daily reality of this can reveal. It's fine for a woman to wish for a husband who will stay home with the kids and support her career, but what if that woman then wakes up one morning resenting her husband for it?

Now imagine how he feels.

Many women are becoming the primary providers for their families. Many men are becoming the primary caregivers to their children.

Amidst all this, is there some vast retrogressive emotional and sexual narrative that exists in direct conflict with the modern request for men to "be more emotional and engaged"? Do some women struggle with what Mundy calls the emotionally retrograde side; yearning for a more traditional man even as they seek an egalitarian marriage?

We are asking men to self-reflect and let go of their own retrogressive cultural conditioning. The question of what traditional conditioning women still carry should come into question at the same time.

It begs a larger conversation.

On "Sensitive" Men and Boys

Lately, I've seen a number of well-written and thoughtful articles about what are being called *highly sensitive men*. The 20 percent or so of men who, in theory, pick up on lots more information from the world around them. These articles represent an effort to create space in our culture for men who show pronounced empathy for others and manifest a wider range of male gender roles, such as caretaking.

All very important and very necessary; all very fine and good. Now, Google "sensitive man" and look at the images that come up:

What you get is pictures of men *crying*. You get pictures of men looking miserable. Distraught. Anxious. As if the very process of being aware or expressive is the instantaneous emotional equivalent of not getting picked for kickball. Where I come from, the kid who didn't fit in was called "a little bit sensitive" by his mom. It was not a positive thing. It was a general apology for a son who couldn't stop cringing during batting practice.

But don't take my word for it. Let's look at the *Merriam-Webster*

Online Dictionary's (https://www.merriam-webster.com) definition of sensitive:

> Sensitive: highly responsive or susceptible: such as ...
>
> 1) easily hurt or damaged; especially ... easily hurt emotionally.
>
> 2) delicately aware of the attitudes and feelings of others

How is it that empathic men have been collectively tagged with a term that defines them as easily hurt emotionally, or delicately aware? How did the word sensitive suddenly become *the term* for these men? Language is a powerful thing. You might as well be calling them "special" and dropping your voice slightly when you say it.

We are very close to pathologizing emotional awareness in men. Because we continue to insist that thick-skinned, emotionally distant men are the baseline for masculinity. (You can thank the Man Box for that helpful discourse.) But emotionally reserved men are a product of their environment, not some kind of genetic inevitability. Why do these emotionally distant men get to be the baseline against which "sensitive men" are judged?

Don't get me wrong. Most articles extoll the virtues of highly sensitive men. Why you should date one. Why you should get one as your nanny. But the language we are using is framing these guys as fragile, as if the capacity for emotional connection is a one-way ticket to anxiety for men.

Moreover, as much as these sensitive guys are being promoted as better husband material, there is still the ongoing subtext that women want a sensitive guy at home while they go party with the bad boys. Grotesquely, our cultural narrative about sensitive men undermines male emotional awareness as a recipe for being taken advantage of by women.

And so, we end up with yet another damaging binary. (God, we love those in American culture.) In this case, we are at risk of creating a false masculine binary that places over-emotional weepers on one end, and bull-in-the-china-shop alpha males on the other, which does a disservice to men across the spectrum of our gender. I would suggest that all men have a capacity for sensitivity and emotional expression. Some just choose not to engage it. They turn it off and for good reason.

So how about we change the whole conversation? How about we frame empathy as a natural expression of male strength; a sign of a more emotionally stable and capable man? Or better yet, let's just pull out all the stops and make the capacity for emotional connection central to being thought of as a fully realized man. Because the idea that only a limited number of men are "highly sensitive" reinforces yet again the damaging view of emotionally closed off masculinity as normative.

The question we should be asking is "for men, what is true strength?" The positive aspect of the highly sensitive man narrative isn't about sensitivity at all. It's about intentional awareness, a simple choice by any man who is willing, to care about what is going on in the emotional lives of the people around him.

If a man chooses not to value empathy, it is most likely because he was not raised to see how central it is to living a fully engaged life. The result is men who are isolated behind a wall of emotional disconnection. Men who are out of touch with their own emotions often self-medicate, leaning heavily on food, sex or drugs.

But boys and men can make a very different choice. They can choose to activate that most central of their human capacities: the ability to connect with and value the emotions of others.

It is a choice that results not in sorrow and fragility but in laughter, connection and play. Moreover, it creates resiliency, community, capacity and strength; strength to weather the challenges of life and to help those they love do so as well. These men are not "delicately aware." They are not "easily hurt or damaged." They have made a choice to be strong.

Men and Emotional Self-amputation

Many American men do a curious thing, especially when we are young. We seek out a romantic partner, form a relationship and then immediately start tracking our partner's responses to what they are learning about us. This is because we are often ashamed of who and what we are.

We take even the slightest indications of confusion or uncertainty in our partner as reason to suppress those parts of ourselves that we fear might not be a good fit for them.

The degree to which men are ready to suppress intimate sides of ourselves as automatically warranting disapproval is a staggering testament to the power of shame in our lives. Our culture's voracious appetite for condemning difference leaves men little flexibility in how they live their lives. In order to avoid being shamed, a man who dreams of being sexually submissive may choose to never share this with his partner. Or a man who is inclined toward family life instead of professional pursuits may still go to the office every day of his life. American men are trapped in a narrow definition of how to perform masculinity. Breaking out can be hugely challenging. This applies to even the smallest aspects of our lives.

If you doubt this, see what happens to the average American man who wears bright pink socks for a day. See how many microaggressions and shaming moments arise. This may be the land of the free, but most of us aren't even free to pick our own socks.

When American men don't share their more intimate aspirations, it is an intense and ongoing process of self-editing that is playing out.

We self-edit because when we do share details of our hidden emotional landscapes, we often find our partners unable to manage the challenges these revelations can create. This is because, as a society, men and women alike have never developed the capacities we need to navigate and explore these landscapes with each other. It takes a partner of significant emotional capacity to manage the flood of emotions that can emerge when men or women are free to reveal their hidden emotional sides.

And so, herein lies the great tragedy of the culture of shame. It is an insidious mechanism for shutting down whole areas of possibility before they ever have a chance to be explored. As men, we surrender the field without a fight. Instead of braving the unknown, and working through the miscommunication that often marks new relationships, men quickly jump to culturally acceptable scripts, in a panic to affirm that we can successfully perform masculinity in approved ways.

These scripts include a range of stereotypes such as:

- Man as provider
- Man as decisive
- Man as having the final word
- Man as sexually aggressive
- Man as emotionally stoic
- Man as straight
- Man as sports focused

Men assume that women want these aspects in us, even as women assume men aspire to perform them. Women, like men, are victims of the same sets of cultural expectations, miscommunications, fears and shame. Accordingly, the conversations about richer alternatives don't take place. It is in this way that the culture of shame collectively enforces conformity and control over us all.

Having been shamed, often as children, men have learned to suppress whatever is within us that does not conform to prevailing cultural standards. Precisely because we have been shamed, for us, everything we are is suspect. We can only imagine someone wanting us *in spite of* our secret needs and aspirations, never *because* of them. The culture of shame suppresses our capacity to value what is good, strong and loving in our distinctness.

Accordingly, men eventually become discouraged with our narrowly defined relationships, moving on to the next, and the next, each time self-editing. We bury the non-normative parts of ourselves that are pathways to a richer more fully engaged life. It is this shame-driven cycle of self-suppression that contributes to the vast sense of disconnection and isolation so indicative of modern American life.

And when we witness someone who is breaking out of gender or sexual stereotypes, we rush to shame and punish them, because they threaten to dig up the forbidden sides of ourselves that we have buried, alone and unmarked, in a potter's field somewhere. It is the self-suppression of men's desires and aspirations that often contributes to epidemic levels of male anger and reactivity, depression, alcoholism, domestic violence, divorce and suicide.

We end up slogging through our days, trapped in the limiting confines of the Man Box. And no amount of religion, sex, sports, financial success, or cultural conformity will address the gap this creates in us. It is a gap between ourselves and the vibrant, unpredictable and celebratory life that eludes us.

And now for the good news: Can we, as men, overcome the drumbeat of shame in our daily lives? The answer is yes. And here's how.

Dr. Saliha Bava, a New York-based couple and family therapist, has a simple and powerful answer for men who are dealing with the culture of shame – *talk about it*:

Shame thrives on confusion and misunderstanding. When you illuminate shame by talking about it, its power diminishes. When we talk about shame, as shame, we can explore it and bring our more private aspirations forward. Once we learn to speak about those aspirations, we can become more comfortable doing so in an ongoing way.

Shame is also deeply personal. We cannot know what others view as shaming unless we talk with them about it. And this includes our friends, wives, husbands, parents and children.

When we talk openly about the culture of shame, the activity of talking shifts the culture. In the moment we speak, we change our path forward.

When we talk openly about the culture of shame, the activity of talking shifts the culture. In the moment we speak, we change our path forward. Change our lives. We have the power to replace the culture of shame with something new that is getting created. What I choose to create is called the culture of permission. You may want to choose something different. Perhaps, for you, it is a culture of compassion, or a culture of adventure.

As couples and families, we can create these conversational spaces in which we talk with curiosity about what shame is for us as individuals. We can create spaces for listening. Create spaces for difference.

These are meant to be ongoing conversations that weave in and out of our daily talk. As part of this, we can help ourselves identify moments of shaming. We can learn to spot shame when it appears. Once we see shame for what it is, we can identify it throughout our lives and guard against letting it have a hold on us.

Dr. Bava's point is clear. If men don't talk about the messages we give and get; if we don't clarify our aspirations for ourselves, the culture of shame will, by default, define our lives for us.

So, let's start pushing back against the culture of shame by bringing our full emotional selves out of the shadows and into the light. Let's make the choice to talk about what we truly want and need in our relationships, and let's start by talking with the people we love most.

Men Who Police and Punish

In 2014, New York Mets baseball player Daniel Murphy chose to take parental leave. The resulting debate swamped the internet. The overheated discussion seesawed between angry condemnations of Murphy's decision to attend the birth of his baby and equally vehement support for his choice. It played out on every major broadcast network and every morning sports page.

Murphy made a decision that is unusual for a professional athlete and because professional sport is the holy grail of American masculinity, Murphy took a beating for his choice. Mostly this beating came in the form of newspaper articles quoting outraged fans because, well, they're fans. And fans are supposed to be ignorant hotheaded idiots. That's why we love them, right? Sports page editors can smile and say, "Hey, we're just reporting the news."

Meanwhile the attack on Murphy's parental leave choice grew. Emboldened by the uproar, nationally known sports commentators mocked Murphy's choice on sports radio, triggering a second backlash in support of Murphy.

I think the backlash against the backlash surprised some people in the man-centric sports world. To those who support Murphy's choice, I say *thank you*.

But this high-profile policing and ensuing cultural firefight around one man's personal decision raises a much bigger question. How much policing of this kind is aimed at men every day? How many macro- and microaggressions are used every hour to control men? To make them behave like "real men." Just how bad is it?

I'll tell you how bad it is. It's worse than any of us will admit.

And men are so used to adjusting to accommodate this crap we hardly notice we're doing it. A sideways glance here, a raised eyebrow there, it doesn't take much to signal when we're failing to act like real men. We have to watch what we say, how we speak, how we walk, point, and gesture, what we discuss, how we dress, what we drive, who we date and how we greet, address and express affection for the people in our lives.

Men in America are subject to an endless list of stringent parameters from within which we are expected to perform masculinity. All of us, every single man in America, lives with the same set of asinine rules that has come to be called the Man Box. For us men, these rules are diligently policed and enforced by the other men, women and even children in our lives. In our "boys wear blue, girls wear pink" world, children begin enforcing these rules by the time they are in kindergarten. If you're a man, wear a pink shirt in front of your first grader and see how quickly you hear about it.

The Man Box specifies a mind-numbing array of rules for being a real man including:

- Real men do not talk about their emotions, except for anger
- Real men are breadwinners not caregivers
- Real men play sports and support sports teams
- Real men are able bodied and physically strong
- Real men are hetero-normative and sexually dominant in the bedroom
- Real men are leaders and have the final word in any discussion
- Real men are never unemployed
- Real men are never uncertain or in need of help

Men who choose (or are forced) to reside in the Man Box are the first to talk about freedom and personal liberty. The fact that they are living within the mind-numbingly narrow perimeters of the Man Box is so deeply ironic that it boggles the mind.

Men who follow the rules of the Man Box are anything but free.

Seriously, position your wrist the wrong way and you're labeled as homosexual. Hold your son if he cries on the playground and you're making him a wimp. And God forbid you publicly or even privately express uncertainty, sorrow or fear. In that moment, you have failed those who depend on you to be unerringly strong, stoic and dependable.

And here's the dirty little secret of men in the Man Box. Even though they never express it, and may not even be fully aware of it, men who live in the Man Box live in fear. They conform emotionally and socially because the prospect of being kicked out of the Man Box is terrifying for them.

It's important to note that traditional masculinity isn't the problem. For many men, traditional masculinity is a good fit. The Man Box isn't about choosing to be a traditional man. You're only in the Man Box when you seek to enforce traditional manhood on others through bullying and intimidation. Sadly, a lot of men make that choice.

The abusive policing of men's behavior even inside the Man Box is brutal. The pecking order is relentless. The jockeying for position goes on night and day. There is no equality there. You're either on top or trying to get there. It's a lifelong hamster wheel that never stops turning. And yet, it is all some men know. It is their only world.

- Am I earning enough?
- Is my wife beautiful enough?
- Am I competitive enough?
- Am I in good enough shape?
- Is my son tough enough?
- Am I surrounded by men who are doing manhood right?
- Am I enforcing the rules of manhood often enough?
- Will the others reject me if they find out my secrets?

Once you have spent a few years in the Man Box, it can become the only way you know to live. Some of these men never learn how to express their emotions. They do not know how to engage people who are different. They rely exclusively on the rules of the Man Box and the fear of expulsion it inspires. And that is how the Man Box controls men. By threatening any man who does not conform with expulsion; forcing them to suppress any part of themselves: sexual, social, racial, professional, or otherwise that does not fit the mold of "real manhood."

Which begs the question. Who is truly tough, brave, and courageous? Those who conform within the Man Box, suppressing their own individuality and punishing others, or those who reject the Man Box and live with all the personal and professional risk of attack that implies?

I have no problem with any man who chooses to perform masculinity in what is thought of as traditional ways. Any man can make this choice and not be in the Man Box. You are only in the Man Box if you enforce this view of manhood as the *only acceptable version.* The days of a single monolithic view of manhood in America are already passing. America is becoming more diverse. The Man Box is coming apart at the seams. But it is still a powerful force.

Meanwhile, if you are living in the Man Box, bullying others to conform, you are not free. Every time you attack another for not behaving the way you think a real man should, you become less free. When you attack a gay man. When you attack a guy who is overweight, or a kid who can't quite kick a football. When you attack a man who's got a strange accent. When you attack a person because of the color of his skin. And yes, when you attack a sports figure for wanting to attend his baby's birth. Every time you do this, you become less free. More trapped. A rat in a cage. A dog on a chain. A prisoner.

The rigid Man Box agenda is never going to make any man happy or truly at peace. It will only make a few men at the top of this abusive societal pyramid scheme rich. And as we all know, even very rich men can be some pretty miserable bastards. Apparently, it's an ugly revelation, finding out that the top of the heap provides little in the way of emotional security. Just more distrust of why and how humans interact. Why is this person talking to me? What do they want? What are they after?

Please, choose to be a traditional American man if that is how you want to perform masculinity, that's fine. But it's not the only way to be a man. There are many ways, too many to count. And in the moment you ditch the idea that everyone has to be like you, you free all of us, including yourself.

Glancing versus Staring

I live in New York City where, when I walk down the street, I see thousands of women a month walking towards and past me. Women of all ages, shapes and sizes. The range of interactions has some variability, but 95 percent of the time, it works like this.

Many of the women I glance at are intentionally not looking at me. They are avoiding all eye contact, seemingly staring into some specific spot on the street that does not contain a man's eyes. If they glance and notice I'm looking at them, they look away very quickly. What I see in that moment is someone being careful. Very, very careful.

I glance at women. I don't look at them for more than a second or two. I never stare at them. I glance at them because they are lovely, or interesting, or fashionable, or simply in my path. I glance at them for the same reasons I glance at men: to judge their intention as they approach me, to see if they're texting instead of looking, to insure I don't get run over.

Because I have a solid sense of who I am and what my intention is, I glance at women without the feeling of guilt or nervousness I carried as a teenager. There is nothing wrong with a glance. But to look longer at a woman you do not know, or to stare? That is a different thing. For the very same reason I do not make and hold eye contact with men (or, for that matter, dogs I don't know) I do not look overly long at women, because it suggests an intrusion; something for which I do not have permission.

When I see any woman walking down the street, avoiding all eye contact, I feel a deep sense of empathy. Accordingly, I don't look for more than a second and I don't let my gaze linger. I do all these things out of respect for a simple fact – women don't feel safe. No matter how "civilized" we insist Western society has become, there is still a high degree of real and present danger for women from aggressive male strangers. And if a woman is from another part of the world, the likelihood that she has faced violence and aggression from male strangers is dramatically higher.

For the record, I track men much more carefully than I do women and for exactly the same set of reasons that women do, because men like to project power. And some men, a very few, like to project power by verbally or physically abusing strangers.

And before you take that deep breath and launch into a list of the ways that men are victims of rape and physical violence from aggressive female partners, don't bother. I have written about that fact numerous times. I'll write about it again right here. The Centers for Disease Control and Prevention's *National Intimate Partner and Sexual Violence Survey 2010 Summary Report*, page 2, states:

> More than 1 in 3 women (35.6%) and more than 1 in 4 men (28.5%) in the United States have experienced rape, physical violence, and/or stalking by an intimate partner in their lifetime.

Yes, men face a range of risks and threats in the world. But as a man, I have never had to live in fear that if I hold eye contact for too long with a woman I do not know, she will approach me and start an unwelcome conversation that could lead to abusive behavior. Why? Because on some level, I always felt I could stand my ground physically. If I had to, I could fight a woman and get away.

But being able to fend off an unwelcome advance is not a certainty for many women. The percentage of men who are abusive in their behavior on the street, in bars, at schools, or in other public places may be limited, but there are enough men out there who behave like this that there is a very real corresponding fear for women; namely, a stranger who won't take no for an answer. For women, it is as follows: Acknowledge a strange man in even the slightest way, get approached. Say, "No thank you" and get shamed, verbally abused, or possibly physically assaulted.

As human beings, we all face a basic challenge. We have to go out into the world and communicate our availability as a potential partner, attract the attention of individuals we view as viable and not attract the attention of individuals we don't find appealing. Doing this in the world is no easy task. It's like trying to garden prize orchids in the middle of a rugby match. And the more you signal your assets as a potential partner, the more attention you attract from persons whose attention you are not seeking.

But a woman's effort to appeal to a prospective mate, whether that be through style of dress or public behavior is not, and should never be, an invitation for unwanted attention. If you are a man in the market for a relationship, take note. The signals and the cues are simple. The rules are even simpler: glance, do not stare. If you get a glance back, look a bit more. If women say "No thanks" in any way (and yes, that can be as simple as glancing away), move on with courtesy and respect.

The vast percentage of men are decent-hearted and would never harm a soul. But some men (and women) are not. Any man who continues to approach women who are indicating "No thank you" in stronger and stronger terms, is being abusive. And as long as there is widespread abusive behavior by a limited number of men in the world, the rest of us will all be forced to limit our social interactions with women in order to try and make the world feel a little safer. Which is a shame.

So, thanks to the jerks of the world for that.

You've made the rest of us men have to prove on a daily basis that we are not you. (Like I wanted to spend my life proving that.) But that's the way it is. And men need to acknowledge that fact, both in their interactions and their political dialogues. Work for change but acknowledge the ongoing facts of the world.

As a person who supports a robust and honest discussion of men's issues, I acknowledge that men face many cultural inequities and challenges. I believe that we need to ensure that men enjoy equal rights in the realms of family law, victim services and other areas. I fully realize that men fall victim to rape and abuse by women. But that does not change the simple math of upper body strength and social conditioning. It is not white knight behavior to advocate for a culture of civility and non-violence toward women. It is simple common decency.

Equally, in the public dance of finding a partner, women may have to become more assertive in indicating interest. Making the first move and communicating clearly when they would like to have a conversation would go a long way to alleviate the concern that men are expected to approach women who give only the slightest nod of interest. This subtle signaling sets men up to face an endless string of rejections, unable to differentiate between the lingering glance that signals interest and the passing glance that does not.

But ultimately, it is the inequity of physical strength that is at the root of our culture's relationship challenges. Most men can simply overpower women. And a small percentage of men do so with terrible consequences. This is what drives some women's anger and fuels the distorted and angry battle between the sexes. Until all of us men, every single one of us, take responsibility for our public and private behavior, all the inequities we face will remain as secondary issues, held hostage by the men among us who behave like animals instead of human beings.

The Suppression of Men's Issues

Is Brutality Toward Women Getting Worse? Recently, I wrote a quick post in response to the story of a child bride in Afghanistan who finally received justice from an Afghanistan court of law.

There were comments on the post from men who wanted to know why I was highlighting "women's issues" yet again, presumably, at the expense of men and boys. Their argument, which is valid on some levels, goes as follows: We have over the last fifty years focused huge amounts of our global resources on women's issues. Legislation, funding, scholarly work, and media discourses have focused on the challenges faced by women both in the U.S. and abroad. Substantive progress has been made.

But has this ongoing focus on women's issues come at the expense of men's rights as fathers, husbands, workers and as victims of violent crimes and rape, as perpetrated both by men and women? Furthermore, are we continuing to feed a cultural dialogue that puts boys and men at a disadvantage in every stage of our societal discourse?

For example: CDC statistics show that women are nearly as likely to be physically abusive in intimate relationships as they are to be abused. Is this fact shared openly by the mass media or shunted aside in favor of narratives that define men as abusers and women as victims?

It is clear to me that we live in a world full of angry, binary discourses. As such, there are ample reasons why people do everything they can to tilt focus to their issues. In the case of women's issues, some percentage of people may have done so in ways that are ultimately harmful to men.

Here's an obvious example. In our culture, if a man strikes his wife and she reports it, the consequences can be immediate and catastrophic for that man. If a woman strikes her husband, and he reports it, are the results as significant? Or is he viewed culturally by the cop on the beat as somehow lacking something integral to being a man? Is he viewed as weak? And are weak men viewed as less deserving of legal recourse than women who, by definition, are defenseless? In a nutshell, the cops (as representatives of our culture's most blunt social priorities) may have very clear training and orders on how to deal with a husband beating his wife. But what training has he or she had to deal with a wife beating her husband? And so, they take a report and walk away shaking their heads.

I can tell you that I have seen this imbalance around physical abuse play out first person. A very kind and gentle friend of mine had the side of his face clawed open by his wife on the day of their son's first birthday. He was unable to attend the party because of this. When I saw him days later he showed me the claw marks on his face. This was a serious wound.

My friend made one thing perfectly clear. He knew that if he did anything in the moment to retaliate physically, he would lose access to his son. He took physical abuse from his wife for years before the marriage finally failed. And he never raised his hand back. But the knowledge that a double standard exists was never far from his mind or mine. When the marriage ended he was stuck holding the alimony and child support bill. I would not relate a story like this if it were not the god's honest truth. The stakes are too high here; the implications too immense.

What we are talking about is the result of a tilted public discourse, in which women's issues have been successfully highlighted (and justifiably so) and in which men remain victims-in-hiding of a range of issues. We have had the first half of the conversation. It's time for the second half to begin.

But is there ill will at work here, intentionally suppressing a public discourse on male issues? I want to address the question of whether or not women's issues have purposely been (and continue to be) highlighted in a way specifically intended to disempower men, because I believe this question lies at the heart of the high level of reactivity from some men's rights advocates.

It would be naive to deny that some of us have bought into the gender wars. There will be numerous examples of incidental smoking guns on all sides. Some people will focus on these kinds of "evidence" to somehow prove an orchestrated effort to suppress men's issues. No matter what side you're on, there will always be examples of the intention to mislead and take advantage of the larger dialogue. Especially when there are vast amounts of public money at stake. But I believe our stunted and contentious discourse about men's issues is mostly the result of long-standing male cultural norms.

Our male cultural history, the steps we took to get here, made ignoring boys and men as victims a likely outcome. Only now are we starting to talk about men as being equally in need of society's focus and resources. Imagining such an idea even twenty years ago would have been impossible, in part, because men refused to think of themselves as needing help. Whatever we have had to endure, the overriding cultural message was, endure it in silence.

Our current living generation of men, born from the 1920s on, spent decades responding to the world in either the angry or confident-macho modes. These were the two acceptable modes of expression by men when confronted with life's challenges. I suppose you can also toss in blind stinking drunk. But the fact is, there was no space in which men could express fear, or weakness, or talk about the abuse in their lives.

In my father's generation there was absolutely no space to discuss men as powerless victims. If things were bad you were expected to just punch back harder. "If you are too weak or stupid to avoid being a victim then it's your own fault" seemed to be the prevailing wisdom. Never mind that some of us were just little children when bad things happened. Being tough was the answer to everything. And not that much has changed.

"Shake it off, crybaby." When we hear that kind of language at the local park, it's always directed at a boy.

The fact is women in our culture have been granted permission to show weakness, to present as victims who need protection. (Even as they are, in some cases, victimizing men.)

But this discourse of victimhood is new for men. This space we have created in which to share our stories and our pain has no long cultural or historical roots. For men, it goes back maybe one generation and it stops.

This is not a discussion I would ever expect to have with my father. These are new ways of speaking for men, and the stories that come pouring out are painful, angry and grief-stricken. They create rage and they cause us to lash out.

Men's sense of being trapped can happen in part because of the backlash we experience when we do share our pain. The cultural rules about men showing weakness are deeply embedded in us and in those we share our beds with. Sometimes the strictest silencers are those closest to us. They prefer the old model. They don't like scary stories and fear. Men are supposed to protect them from that.

Sharing the stories of our victimhood is a double-edged sword. Victimhood is a toxic state and one has to move past it or risk being drained and weakened by the very forces we are in opposition to. If we, as men (or women), are empowered to tell publicly how we have been victimized, we should be wary of becoming trapped in that story of our victimhood.

Some men and women in our culture would make a lifelong mission out of their victimhood. Demanding acknowledgement over and over again without giving much consideration to their responsibilities to society at large. They batter and attack others, brandishing their victimhood like a club. But they are the price we pay for a wider, more open discourse.

If men and boys are finally emerging from that place in which we have been prohibited from telling our painful stories, then this represents a shift of historic proportions. Because in telling these stories we can find common ground with others, and we can highlight how the old, stale narratives about what it is to be a man not only fall short but also are grossly divisive, abusive and unfair.

I would suggest that telling our stories is possible now. Not everywhere and not all the time. But we have our foot in the narrative door and we're not taking it out. And if we want our fair share of the resources and energy directed at growing a better world, we should start looking for common ground around all the stories being told by men or women alike.

The Emptiness of Male Friendships

Imagine, Frank walks into a bar. He approaches a group of men from work, including someone new. One guy says, "Frank, meet Bob." They all chat for a while and then Frank says brightly, "Bob! I'm glad I met you. I like you. How would you like to be my friend?" Cue the abuse and derision because Frank just broke the "don't ask, don't tell" rule of male friendship. Don't admit you want or need friends. Don't admit you need anything. Be confident. Be self-reliant.

Will you be my friend? Sometime around first grade, boys stop asking that question and they never ask it again, because it quickly becomes an invitation for bullying and abuse. Stop and think about that for a moment. This single observation, that men are taught to deny they want and need friends, lies at the core of everything that is wrong with our modern construction of manhood. And it is killing us.

Judy Chu's research, as documented in her book, *When Boys Become Boys*, has shown that boys are taught to perform this narrative as early as age four.

Researcher and author of *Deep Secrets*, Niobe Way has this to say about the cultural conditioning of boys and men:

Boys know by late adolescence that their close male friendships, and even their emotional acuity, put them at risk of being labeled girly, immature, or gay. Thus, rather than focusing on who they are, they become obsessed with who they are not – they are not girls, little boys nor, in the case of heterosexual boys, are they gay. In response to a cultural context that links intimacy in male friendships with an age, a sex (female), and a sexuality (gay), these boys mature into men who are autonomous, emotionally stoic, and isolated.

Welcome to American manhood, where only if you don't need friends will you be worthy of having them.

There is a reason most American men would never ask another man directly to enter into a friendship. Boys and men in American culture are given little opportunity in life to master this kind of interpersonal risk taking. It creates a moment of uncertainty that is agonizing for men. To ask for friendship suggests vulnerability, flexible social standing or even willingness to admit need. All values that are roundly condemned in men.

Instead of connecting in emotionally authentic ways, American men are taught from an early age to access friendships obliquely by joining clearly defined groups, teams or organizations. The opportunities for social contact arise in Boy Scouts, on baseball teams or in schools. This kind of social organizing aligns large populations of boys, teaching them to follow clear and simple rules of how to perform being a boy. Some organizations actually provide written handbooks, manuals by which to determine rank, achievement, behavior and appropriate forms of expression. The Boy Scout handbook is one obvious example.

Within these organizations, even social stragglers are grudgingly allowed to remain part of the group regardless of their individual standing. Quickly, boys learn to self-select their rank and standing. Alphas at the top, socially awkward boys at the bottom. Boys learn that advancing in the organization doesn't require the higher relational skills of tracking nuance or holding uncertainty. Social risk taking is not rewarded. Being on top simply requires the application of confidence and assertion and a willingness to perform masculinity according to what is normative.

In this way, boys are taught to express a simplified social identity by virtue of their organizational associations. By extension, friendships formed in these organizations are also expressed in restricted and simplified ways. They are friendships that encourage conformity and avoid interpersonal authenticity.

In adulthood, men continue to seek friends in the safe but highly conforming contexts of work, team sports, church, or their wives' social or familial connections. They become friends with the parents they meet at the PTA. They rely on the Lions Club, fraternity or their son's scout troop. They connect by way of organizations, tracking and performing friendship in the ways that are collectively deemed to be appropriate.

Because their friendships are sourced in organizations, men can end up keeping much of their uniqueness hidden and cleave close to what is culturally normative for those institutions. This creates a high degree of homogeneity in how men express, engage and perform friendship. Joe is my friend because Joe comes to bowling every week, not because Joe is necessarily someone I connect with on any other level.

These risk-free friendships are based solely on proximity. They require that men hide any atypical aspects of their internal narratives. This leaves men feeling emotionally isolated, providing no social mechanisms for men to process the challenges in their lives. Organizational conformity guarantees belonging at the expense of authentic self-expression. The result? We end up alone in a crowd.

Which is why for men, when their participation in any given organization ends, the relationships or friendships embedded in those organizations often end as well. Emotional authenticity is the glue that holds friendships together. Without it, they are too shallow and fragile to survive beyond simple convenience.

In the absence of the expression of our emotional authenticity, American men become homogeneous in their expression of self. This encourages their location, willingly or otherwise, in the Man Box, within its set of rigid expectations that define what a "real man" is, particularly in American culture.

A real man is strong and stoic. He doesn't show emotions other than anger and excitement. He is a breadwinner. He is heterosexual. He is able-bodied. He plays or watches sports. He is the dominant participant in every exchange. He is a firefighter, a lawyer, a CEO. He is a man's man. This "real man," as defined by the Man Box, represents what is supposedly normative and acceptable within the tightly controlled performance of American male masculinity.

Men will ask women to have sex and take a "no" without skipping a beat. Men will ask a customer to buy a product and take "no" as just part of the territory. But asking another man to "please be my friend" represents social risk-taking that's guaranteed to end badly because, in the moment a man asks this question, he has failed to be what all men are expected to be. He has failed to be, and pay close attention to the word I'm using here, competent.

Men move in circles of competence. This competency component is central to how men are ranked in the institutions they rely on for social connection: in sports, at work and in every garage and backyard barbecue in the country. We approach each other not just in terms of common interests, but in terms of our competency in those areas. "Knowing how" determines status, and men are highly focused on status in the larger pecking order of traditional manhood.

We approach with our personal relationships wired tight and fully formed. We are successful, smart, aggressive, opinionated and full of advice on what's wrong with the world and how to correctly do what needs to be done. By extension, we already have plenty of friendships that spring fully formed into our lives, born magically out of our authority and status.

This nearly universally approved cultural dynamic between men creates an entirely different outcome with women.

Men are taught to validate themselves with other men by fostering the impression that they always know exactly what they're talking about. But this focus on competence, the transactional coin for tracking and assigning status between men, becomes something entirely different when employed with women. Been wondering where *mansplaining* comes from? It comes from right there. It's not men thinking they know everything. Its men's fear that they will fail to give that impression and be shamed for it. It comes from the transactional nature of male relationships.

The male focus on competence and social status is tied to our belief that our chances of success in business and personal interactions increase when underpinned by something we can leverage. Our position in the company. Our financial success. Our skill at golf. Our willingness to advance the goals of the organization. Something other than individual, distinctive selves.

We lead with: "You'll want to be my friend because I have something you need, not because of who I am." And men carry this same dynamic into their romantic relationships, often leading with the "good provider" story. It's why we pay for dinner on the first date. It's rooted in opening doors and providing service to women because somewhere deep down, we're just not enough without the financial or service element. Or worse, because we want to hold various forms of leverage in any relationship we enter.

Either way, it's ultimately about male insecurity. Male insecurity born out of the fact that we have never been taught to lead with our own authentic emotional selves.

Seeking friendship by offering what others can leverage is the central transactional skill boys are taught from childhood. Buying our way in, instead of offering who we are as human beings, sets up a circular pattern by which men are always expected to bring, contribute, produce, provide.

Collectively, we are raising men to feel insecure unless they can bring their transactional leverage. It's a lesson we were not taught by the women we date as adults, but by the boys we were first grouped with as children. That said, men and women alike participate in this generational cycle of transactional intimacy. It's pay to play.

So, we take our personal stories off the table and put our competence, our networks and our alpha narratives up front. But here's the challenge. If our friendships are exclusively about confidence and competence, then by definition, they cannot be authentic, because no one is competent across the board. No one is completely without uncertainty or confusion.

When we share our uncertainty, we start asking much bigger questions. It is in those conversations that we speak with honesty and authenticity, creating opportunities to form connection, change and grow. Boys and men are not taught to leverage these powerful capacities. In fact, they are taught to avoid them as signs of weakness or indecision.

The result is an epidemic of isolation.

A 2010 study by AARP revealed that one in three Americans aged 45 and older are chronically lonely. Up from one in five just ten years before. That's 44 million Americans.

In an article for *The New Republic* titled "The Lethality of Loneliness," Judith Shulevitz writes:

Emotional isolation is ranked as high a risk factor for mortality as smoking. A partial list of the physical diseases thought to be caused by or exacerbated by loneliness would include Alzheimer's disease, obesity, diabetes, high blood pressure, heart disease, neurodegenerative diseases, and even cancer. Tumors can metastasize faster in lonely people.

Men's friendships can feel shallow and transitory because so many of their relationships are lacking in emotional authenticity. Emotional authenticity is the glue that holds deeper, more long-term friendships together. Men who find themselves surrounded by risk-free, surface-level friendships can end up isolated, especially in the event of life challenges like losing a job or getting divorced. The absence of a robust circle of friendships in men's lives contributes directly to epidemic levels of stress-related illnesses, depression, suicide and violence.

How do we counteract our culture of male isolation? We parent with the goal of growing our children's relational capacities. This is all about staying in conversation with them over the years, helping them in the small daily conversations of life to see how powerful their capacities for communication and expression are. It's about getting our children to that tipping point whereby they commit to their own distinctive voice over the scripted silences of traditional manhood.

Our children can grow their relational capacities through conversation and connection within their families with people they trust. It's part of the joyful work of parenting and we can choose to make it a priority on their behalf.

Meanwhile, I, for one, am seeking friendship in more individual and authentic ways. I'm going to look for friends away from simple zones of convenience and proximity. I'm not going to lead anymore with something transactional that I think might be of value. Not my network. Not my business connections. Not my ability to earn approval by conforming to some set of expectations or common goals. Out front of all that, I'm just offering me. Myself. I want to lead with who I am. Getting here took a lot of blood, sweat and tears so I'll be damned if I'm going to be convinced to hide it away.

I want to take risks. I want to be who I'm becoming, and continue to make more authentic, emotionally vibrant friendships with the remarkable men and women I meet in the world.

Put simply, I want to live a good life.

The Sadness Ghost

In the summer of 2011, an 8-year-old boy was murdered here in New York City. He got lost walking the few blocks home from day camp. It's a chilling story, even more so for parents of young children.

When I read about it, my first response was, "I have to get my son away from the city." Close on the heels of that thought came the question of how to get my son – who's six, sweet, full of energy, and talkative – not to trust strangers. What if some guy takes my boy away?

A few days later my son looked down at a newspaper lying on the sidewalk. It read, "Missing Brooklyn Boy Found Murdered" and had a picture of the boy staring up at us. My son, who can read, asked me what it meant. I haltingly explained that someone the boy didn't know killed him. I used simple language and moved through the explanation quickly and in a neutral tone, but I didn't lie. I told him that, sometimes, strangers could be dangerous.

In a quiet voice, he said, "This is bad." And we walked on toward the park.

To this day, I don't know whether it was the right decision to be honest, standing there, looking down at that newspaper. I felt the weight of the world settle on my 6-year-old son and me. It was one of those moments when telling simplified stories or outright lies seems like a much better idea in retrospect.

A few nights later, I found out he had been crying, and that he was sad because of a song on the radio that he'd heard. The song was "American Pie" by Don McLean. You probably know the lyrics:

Bye, bye Miss American Pie / Drove my Chevy to the levee,

but the levee was dry / Them good ol' boys were drinking whiskey and rye, singing / This'll be the day that I die / This'll be the day that I die.

"He's has been crying all evening," his mother told me. (His mother and I are divorced.) "He doesn't want to hear 'American Pie' anymore," she said. I realized that his simple response, *This is bad*," had only been the tip of the iceberg.

A day or so later, our son was talking with his stepmother, Saliha and me. He told her he was very sad. "I've been sad for three days, and I don't want to be sad anymore."

Saliha, who is a couple and family therapist, asked him what was making him sad. He told us he was thinking about death. He then put his hands over his ears, lay down on his side, and shut his eyes. He cried about Olive, our cat that had died a couple of years before. I thought, "I shouldn't have told him about the boy," getting a chill in my gut – the feeling that I'd done something irreversible.

Saliha asked him about his sadness. He said he just couldn't stop feeling sad. He has a little tray full of plastic figures he's been collecting called Toonz. He has about 40 of them. He looked at us and said, "What's the point of collecting things if I'm going to die? What will happen to them when I'm dead?" He repeated that he didn't want to be sad anymore and that he couldn't stop thinking about it.

Saliha said, "Close your eyes and picture something for me. I want you to think about an orange. Can you picture it?"

He said, "Yes."

Saliha said, "OK, now I want you to stop thinking about it."

My sweet son opened his eyes and looked at Saliha. He closed his eyes again. "OK," he said.

"Stop thinking about how the orange peel smells. Stop thinking about how the orange tastes. Don't think about how the peel looks when you tear part of it off."

"I can't stop thinking about it because you keep talking about it!" he yelled, equal parts exasperated and amused.

"OK," said Saliha. "Now think about an apple."

"OK," he said.

"Think about its red color," said Saliha.

"Green," he said. "I like green apples."

"OK," said Saliha, "think about its green color. Think about how it tastes. Think about how crunchy and tart it is." "Now," said Saliha, "can you see the orange?"

"No," he said, amused.

"If you want to stop thinking about something, you can't just tell yourself to stop. You have to think about something else," she said. "You grow what you focus on. So, if you think about sadness, you'll grow sadness. If you think about happiness, you'll grow that. Think of the orange as sadness and the apple as happiness. If you want to stop thinking about the orange, you have to think about something else, about the happiness, about the apple."

Our little boy took the oranges and apples idea and, within a few moments, he'd reassigned ice cream as the happiness thought. We talked about what would be examples of "ice cream thoughts." We talked more about choosing what thoughts we might want to grow so as not to feel sad. Bedtime came, I read him some books, and he went to sleep.

At some point later, Saliha told me that thinking about an emotion, like sadness, over and over may create a groove or a worn path that the mind can get into the habit of traveling.

She then posed the following question: why is sadness necessarily a bad thing? We can hold sadness just like other emotions. It's part of life. Sadness can even be good.

The next morning, he woke and called to me that he'd had a bad dream. "I dreamed that Mommy went away for two years," he told me.

I got him out of his bed and we began our day. We sat at the dining table, which, as usual, was covered in our art supplies. He said Mommy was gone, and it made him sad. I asked him to tell me more about the dream. We talked about sadness and he returned to the subject of his toys and death. He said he didn't want to collect any more toys. What was the use? (A hell of a good existential question, by the way.)

Then something magical happened. It's been a while since that day, and I'm sure I'm not constructing it accurately, but I recently found a page in a journal that I'd flipped open that morning and made notes in as my son was speaking to me.

In preparation for sharing what he said, let me first explain that he and I are both artists. We draw pictures. We often draw them as a way to order our thoughts about the world, or to construct stories that help us experience it.

As we spoke, I asked him again about sadness – not death, but sadness. Saliha's concern that we not try to hide from sadness was on my mind. And then one of us, I don't know which, said, "What if sadness is a cartoon? How would we draw it?"

My son got his pencils and he drew the Sadness Ghost. He was very specific. He drew the eyes several times. I had a second sheet of paper, on which I drew versions of the ghost with different eyes, and he said, "No, Daddy, those aren't right."

The eyes he drew were blank and ghostly, but they're not angry or mean. My son can draw angry and mean eyes. He draws them all the time on his dragons. These eyes were lost, and perhaps worried. But they were also, as he described them, "cute."

In the moment he conceptualized the Sadness Ghost, he activated his own solution for processing what he was feeling. In that moment, he ceased to be a sad person and became, instead, a person who was being visited by sadness. This distinction is crucial in processing powerful, sometimes-overwhelming emotions like rage, fear, or grief.

Together, we created our story for the Sadness Ghost. We talked about being "visited by sadness." We talked about how sadness wasn't always a bad thing; that we all feel sad sometimes.

Then he said, "The Sadness Ghost comes and goes. It's OK for the Sadness Ghost to come. He can come for a little while because he's cute. He comes to me as a hiding place for him because he's scared. But later, he has to go when he's not *too* scared."

This little boy then played the role of himself speaking to the Sadness Ghost. "OK, now go," he said gently, gesturing for the ghost to go, indicating that we each have to know when to tell sadness to move on.

What's remarkable is how he was able to accept sadness into himself in the form of the Sadness Ghost, and then *care for it.*

He became the caretaker of his own sadness; he became the safe place where his sadness could come to be comforted. He no longer defined himself as sad. He was being *visited* by sadness – a very different way to frame the experience.

In the days after that, our son's sadness went away. He went back to collecting things with a vengeance. He moved on to his ice-cream thoughts. And although sadness will visit him many times in his life, I hope his capacity to hold it will remain as vital and powerful as it was that morning.

Biking Manhattan

I just finished a crazy bike ride down Ninth Avenue through midtown Manhattan.

Barreling down the long slope from West 57th, southbound on Ninth Avenue, is to be part of a sun-glare avalanche of surging yellow cabs and pothole-banging delivery trucks jostling through bottlenecked mobs of aimless texting pedestrians. It's funny and crazy and dangerous and I love it. There are moments when I am tracking so many visual variables that the ride becomes a peripheral vision fever dream. You shoot past cabs, people's startled faces visible for the briefest of moments in the passenger window. Who are they? What is their life like? Are they happy?

Ninth Avenue is a symphony of variables, all in motion. Some drivers notice you. Some are oblivious. You have to know which are which. You see the whites of their eyes as they glance at you in the side-view mirrors. Each person texting on each passing corner could be the one. Lady. Pink blouse. Man, black backpack. Kid, smoking. Women, two kids. Baby stroller, no, two baby strollers. Looking. Not looking. Any one of them could be the one that steps off the curb, absentmindedly, just as you are shooting the gap.

I'm 53 years old.

I'm going to miss riding crazy like this. Sometime in the next few years, I'll wake up one day and that will be that. I will still ride my bike but biking Ninth Avenue will recede into yesterday. For me, that part of my life will be finished. It's so tempting to boil aging down into a bleak list of things you can't do any more. It creeps up on you in your forties. Your eyes go, then your joints. It's weird how quickly we adjust to and accept this daily paring away of our physical prowess.

I feel like I'm bidding a long farewell to my younger self. A friend who's gathering his coat and cap to leave. He is lingering at the door now, reluctant to go. But he's got a train to catch. He'll go.

That youthful self is still vibrant within me. And I'm working to bring the essence of him forward in some form, spiritual or otherwise, into tomorrow, a gift to the old man I'll become in fifteen years or so. But who are our younger selves? And how do these energetic, vibrant hungry beings inform us as we age? Can our older selves find connection and continuity with the remnants of youth in us? I can tell you this much, those two selves, young and old, will either be adversaries or partners. I feel my job is to teach them to be friends, before it's too late.

Take drinking for instance. I used to drink a lot. I don't any more. My body simply can't take it. I guess I'm lucky that way. It hurts too much the next day. So, two glasses of wine and I'm done. But I know guys my age who still sit up all night drinking beer. Ten or 12 beers, one after another, until 2 a.m. And I'm left wondering, is the young in them fighting the old? Did the old do something wrong? Are the ways they lived when they were younger, the solutions that gave them joy, reluctant to step aside for something new?

Just as my youth goes, the old man I will be is coming. As much as I'd like to bar the door, he's out there, just raising his hand to knock. I know that knock is coming. I can feel it in my right shoulder. In my knees when I push myself too hard. I feel it when drowsiness creeps over me during a long day. Old age wakes me in the dead of night, worrisome thing that it is.

I used to sleep like a baby. But now I wake sometimes. I lie there and take stock, over and over, like a grocer who can't believe his inventory. Did I order that? Where are my customers? I turn decades-old events and relationships over in my mind. Examining the emotions they give rise to. Regrets wheedle in, money gone wrong, some empty aimless relationship I wasted precious years on, or the woman I should have stayed with. People my age who have already died. People who got famous. As you lie there in the dark, all the pat ideas about success and failure creep up on you. You played your cards wrong somehow.

You can do this 2 a.m. exercise endlessly if you are not careful. You can obsess on a cycle of questions that have no end, because they are the past and the past can be a carnival wheel of garish emotions and old tapes you spin again and again. Eventually, if you're smart, you say, "Don't do that anymore," and you'll let it rest.

Even as age exacts its price, it brings great gifts. If you shift your focus, you'll realize that something remarkable is happening.

With age, over the last few years, I've found that my mind is synthesizing information in startling and deeply satisfying ways. It's as if all the cramming of experience into my head and heart has finally resulted in a reliable mechanism of understanding. It manifests as a higher awareness, very much spiritual in its nature. It manifests as a capacity for calming and ordering one's reactions to the world. It has made me smarter and sweeter and more self-assured. And the source is hard for me to pin down. But I believe it will come to any of us who are actively engaged in life. As if the divine says, "You've done enough struggling to understand. Here, have a glimpse of peace."

I do credit the birth of my son and the years of service I have given him as part of what got me here. My connection to him has made me a more patient, thoughtful and self-assured person. My wife is a huge part of it. Her path has made mine so much more meaningful. The people I have known in my life, the places I have seen, they all play a part. But it's more than any person's influence, or even the map of our choices.

I think, perhaps, we're designed to make a leap in our fifties.

There is clearly a refining of skills that takes place. If you spend a lifetime writing or designing or dancing, or building, the pursuit of your craft as a practice of skill or technique falls away and intuition takes over. It's a synthesis of years of work, resulting in flow. What you have sought to master, thought about, processed for decades becomes transcendent. You hit your best years. You get the payoff.

This is what happens in living, too. If you can turn your attention from what is past, towards the miraculous things that are coming, you will see the patterns of divinity that younger eyes often can't spot. The trappings, appetites, desires and demands of youth are driven by the need to experience life, to accrue data. Once we are gorged on decades of experience, it's time to seek something higher. If you look for it, it is right there, waiting.

I can't say for sure where life will go. What is emerging may work out or it may not. But I can tell you this. Life seems like a huge adventure now. What once was a struggle to make sense of the world now is a glimpse of something peaceful and full of love. I only catch a glimpse of it, this note of peace ... but it's there. I've seen it right there on Ninth Avenue, in the sun-washed faces rushing by.

So, if you're young. Be young. Try not to do any damage if you can help it. But be young. It's your job to take it all in. But if you're wondering about getting older, trust me, the amazing stuff is coming. It's just a matter of being open to it.

A Father's Secret Walk

My son and I discussed Donovan's song, "Atlantis" the other morning as we made our way to school here in Manhattan. We scampered, hopped, pantomimed, declared, performed and anime-ran (bent forward with both arms straight back) our way to the subway. The subject of our ever so important discourse leapt quicksilver from Legos to Donovan to the Atlantic Ocean to Atlantis to myth and time and back to toys.

When I first moved into our apartment, I was a little concerned about the length of the daily walk from 10th Avenue to 8th Avenue, where the subway stop is. He was only five then. And the long "avenue blocks" seemed like quite a journey.

Now, three years later, we have created an entire walking, conversation and play ritual that grows and evolves further and further on any morning that we make the trip. Each storefront and school building has a ramp or a tree around which we circle or stomp. There are zigzags that correspond with specific sets of old, blue paving stones. We declare with great alarm the location of every uncollected dog poop. There are narrow places and wide places.

There are sections of "line up behind me" sidewalk, hemmed in by stoops and bus stop shelters, where older schoolkids pour past. When he was much littler, we had a code. I would squeeze his hand three times in quick succession and he would swing in behind me as I bulled through the press on the sidewalk, my bulk making a path for his little form behind me. Now he weaves his own way through the press, meeting up on the far side, never breaking stride.

At first, I always carried his backpack. Then at some point he began shouldering it himself: books and homework and a lunch kit. Swim trunks, goggles, pencils and a handful of Squinkies. Metro card, library pass, stray buttons and found pennies, rubber bands, and always a collection of drawings. All of these things left my shoulder and they won't be coming back.

Last night, I walked behind him and his Bonus Mom, Saliha, as the two of them took that same walk, telling stories, and moving to the same traveling rhythm on the very same blocks. They talked to each other. And for a short magical time, I became invisible walking behind them.

I felt such peace and such joy to see him sharing his joyful discourse with Saliha. I got to witness, in silence, what it looks like when he engages in the magical walking conversation, which we have all created with him. I caught a secret glimpse of the thousands of other conversations he has had and will have, with the world of other people: his Mom and Bonus Dad, his friends, teachers, people, all over the wide world. A world of conversations we have all helped him to create and love.

So, I walked behind the two of them, as they danced their conversational dance. And I saw the magic of their gift of storytelling and interplay. I saw the legacy I have had a hand in creating for him. It put me at peace. It gave me confidence in his path forward in the world.

For a few more years, I will walk him to school. And we will talk, jump, debate, prepare, and compare. For a few more years, his hand will enter and leave mine twenty times a trip, as natural as can be. When that hand will stop coming for mine I cannot say. But when it stops (if it ever does) I will not grieve the passing of those moments. I make a conscious effort to hold and celebrate these changes each in their turn.

But here and now I have these wonderful days, with his hand coming to rest in mine, warm in the chill of winter. Leaving just as quickly, to transmit a gesture, going up into the air with a flourish, moving with a comforting rhythm all its own. I am at peace. Because I know for a certainty, from my winter night's walk in the darkness behind him, that his conversations will go on, with or without me; that his gift of gab, and our special deeply personal way of talking and laughing and being is his gift now to give to others. I've seen him create these conversations.

And I also know one other thing. I know that I wouldn't want to live right next to the subway stop for all the tea in China.

And that's a lot of tea.

Are Men Changing?

Yesterday, on a conference call with The Good Men Project writers and editors, CEO Lisa Hickey raised a question that would seem to constitute a central issue of our age. It's a question that comes up time and time again in Hickey's work.

A reporter had asked her just a day or two before, "Are men changing?"

At which point, I would be sorely tempted to ask said reporter, "Are women changing?" As if that question is not absurd when asked of any segment of the population. We're all changing.

This question implies that men are all members of some kind of monolithic club where we all sit around in smoking jackets, collectively choosing to change or not based on some secret man club handbook of standards and practices.

From where I sit, men are anything but singular in their nature. They are as vast and diverse a category of creatures as you could ask for. Much like women, in fact. Accordingly, it should be a given that men are equally as fluid, mercurial and ever changing. Changing all the time. Change-y. You see what I'm getting at? "Are men changing?" is, in fact, a very loaded and leading question.

Hickey wanted to discuss the question on our call because she sees the cultural narratives of men refusing to change as being in direct contradiction to what she sees in all the men in her professional and personal life. Hickey goes on to say, "The reality of individual men that I know DOES NOT correspond to the cultural narratives out there."

And yet the question persists.

I have been writing for The Good Men Project for a while now. Since connecting with this vibrant, funny, aggravating and deeply beautiful community of men and women, I have engaged in more conversations about men and manhood than I have had in the previous five decades of my life. These conversations have echoed back down the long corridors of my own history. My time at The Good Men Project has led me back to myself as a small child, a sometimes frightened and confused boy, a rebellious and celebratory young man, a father, a husband and a lover across the many years I have been alive. You can't spend time here and not reflect on your life. It's in the nature of the stories that are told here.

During our conference call, the first frame that arose (and always seems to arise when we talk about men and change) was the impact of corporations and their internal structures as the embodiment of alpha male energy. When we talk about men, we immediately envision great corporate beehives made up of grimly determined males, who are either driving to the top, crushing all beneath them, or slaving away their lives, estranged from their wives and children by the seduction of the fat paycheck. These narratives are presented as clear evidence that men are, in fact, not changing.

And then comes, yapping at the heels of this bleak summation, the ever so popular mass media meme that men STILL don't help enough with the housework. It's almost dark comic relief when compared to the bleak vistas of corporate masculinity. It conjures images of America's women who, having put in their own eighty-hour work week, return home to 100 million husbands reclining on 100 million couches watching 100 million ESPN broadcasts while their babies wail mournfully in darkened kitchens, the scent of dirty diapers wafting on the air-conditioned breeze. It would be funny, if it didn't reinforce over and over the narrative that men are lazy, self-entitled slobs who are universally insensitive to basic ideals of fairness. And, even more poisonous, that women are too weak and victimized to do anything about it.

Sigh. Happy Father's Day, by the way.

So. These are the primary entry points to the discussion on men and change? Really? Yet they come up over and over again. Dirty dishes and corporate shark tanks. And for the record, every man I know (including my 87-year-old father) cleans, washes, launders and cooks on behalf of his family, sharing equally in what continues to be mislabeled as women's work. And yet, no matter how many of us do it, we remain the anomalies, the exceptions that prove the rule. Couch. ESPN. Baby crying ...

My little Father's Day 2013 gift to men everywhere? I'm calling bullshit on that one. If you ladies are with someone who won't do his (or her) fair share of the housework, demand better. It ain't testicles. It's cultural. And that culture is changing, fast. So, stop settling for that kind of behavior. And for the millions of men who are with someone who won't do their fair share of the housework? Ditto. At some point we all have to demand a baseline of fairness from our partners or find better ones. It's not enough to keep blaming the culture at large for the often unspoken agreements we have created in our own lives.

But I digress.

I do understand how these ways of thinking get to be the preeminent frame for men and change. I really do. For one thing, binary frames about housework sell newspapers, elevating catty gendered debates that give cable news anchors something to wax inane about. But there is also a deeper and more fundamental agent at work.

All of us, men and women alike, have the capacity to get lost in the quagmire of the damage in our pasts, repeatedly resurrecting the most painful stories or fears that haunt us. What we once suffered can, paradoxically, become the red and dripping meat that sustains us. We plunge into simplistic black-and-white cultural narratives, seeking the generalizing judgmental memes that echo the damage done to us and we make them our own. In doing so, we reanimate our past abusers back into the world. Reenergizing the frames of victimhood and conflict. Saying, in effect, that these wrongs, large and small, are the central stories of the world.

But they are not the central stories of this wide, beautiful world unless we empower them to be.

We all have suffered abuse, bigotry, abandonment and the many evils of the world. Some of us have suffered much more than others. I do not in any way wish to minimize the trauma of others. But the stories we choose to make central in our lives can, and hopefully will, transcend the traumas we have experienced.

The world needs for us to do this.

Our conversations in The Good Men Project community are about the deepest mysteries of being human; of what it means to speak, cry, hope, hate, lust, love, and die. We talk about the way vast human revolutions, playing out century by century and minute by minute, have impacted us personally. Tying the theoretical to the relational, to the personal, to the spiritual. I remain deeply optimistic about the power of telling these personal stories, because they are changing the world, both for those who tell their stories and for those who hear them.

There is a central truth at work here. Unlike the past wrongs done to us, which cannot be changed, the stories we tell about our lives can change. What we choose to focus on is what we grow in our lives. Said another way, we live the stories we tell. And no matter our circumstances, we retain the power to tell any story in any way we choose, accentuating the markers of joy or reinforcing the symbols of our despair.

I see daily the power of the stories I choose to tell in my own life. When I look down at my own hands, soapy with dishwater, or at my fingers intertwined in my son's exuberant grasp, I feel a perfect note of peace moving through me. I see it in the laughing eyes of my wife. My stories are there.

If I am ever to pray, if that moment is to arrive in my life, it will likely happen as I hold my dear son or darling wife while they drift off to sleep. It will not be a prayer of worry or need or some plea for the future. It will not be a prayer of thanks or satisfaction.

It will be a prayer of the perfect NOW; where every echo of struggle and despair falls silent in the gentle movement of breath. I am a very lucky man. So lucky that I doubt I will ever fully be able to offer the thanks my life deserves. My words would collapse and fall short. And knowing this is, I think, where the first seeds of wisdom lie. Typically, we cannot own the miracles we live. They pass through us. They are the wind that drives us forward. But they remain, essentially, a mystery that we are open to but can never fully grasp.

But occasionally a miracle will make its nature known to us. For me, telling my stories at The Good Men Project has helped me better understand my place in the world. And believe me, that is most certainly a miracle. I hope every man and woman reading this will consider sharing their stories alongside mine. Contact them at https://goodmenproject.com. We need you to tell your personal stories, because when you share your stories the world becomes more diverse, colorful and real. The world becomes more human.

But what about our original question? *Are men changing?*

I believe there is overwhelming evidence that they are, as they move in huge numbers into primary child care, more collaborative relational ways of working and, yes, the wonderful world of cleaning the bathroom. But the bigger question is, as men change, are we updating the stories we carry about men? Or are those stories lagging behind; stalling change by anchoring our view of men to the past? And if so, what can we do about that?

Lisa Hickey said during our conversation yesterday that the challenge we have with men and change lies with our archaic cultural narratives. A society that circulates limited stories of what men are will limit men's choices. She believes that the answer for how to empower men is to share stories of the full range of what men are. It's about creating a cultural wellspring of stories, options and choices for men. If you want to be a CEO, fine. Go ahead. But if you want to be a stay-at-home dad, or anything else you can imagine, dream on, because a vast range of options out there are just as valid as focusing on earning money, or accruing status and power.

What's more, depending on how you define your markers for a rewarding life, you may find you have a better life than the most powerful captains of industry.

The Good Men Project is sharing just these kinds of ideas. Hickey believes that by sharing them we are already moving closer to a cultural tipping point, whereby the idea of what a man can be becomes more diverse, empowered and authentic.

The crappy mass media narratives about men will continue. They will go on telling our sons, brothers and fathers that the way to be a man is through your wallet or your fists. Our responsibility is to add other stories and other ideas to the cultural mix. Yes, men can be tough, focused warriors. But they can also be gentle and loving and playful and funny and sweet and yes, feminine. They can be healers and caregivers and poets and artists and everything else under the sun. And a big part of this equation is to let little girls know all the things that boys can be. So that when those girls grow up to be women, they do not end up enforcing old ideas, but instead are empowered to seek a partner from the full range of what men are, because every man is different. Every man is change. Every man has something inside him that deserves to grow and find its place in the world.

By sharing our stories, we help make that possible.

Why Do We Murder the Beautiful Friendships of Boys?

On a cold February night a few weeks ago, professor and researcher Niobe Way presented findings from her book *Deep Secrets*, here in New York. (Her book is available on Amazon.) She was hosted by Partnership With Children, a groundbreaking organization doing powerful interventions with at-risk children in the New York Public Schools. Way's and Partnership With Children's work have produced reams of hard statistical data proving that emotional support directly impacts every metric of academic performance. And, as it turns out, every other part of our lives as well.

That night, as my wife Saliha and I made our way down the snow-blown streets towards Fifth Avenue, I was feeling the somber weight of the third month of dark Northeast winter, wondering how many days remained until spring would come. "It's February. Don't kid yourself," the answer came back. My charming and lovely wife was to take me to dinner after Way's presentation. It was my birthday.

Niobe Way is Professor of Applied Psychology at New York University and director of the Ph.D. program in Developmental Psychology. A number of years ago, she started asking teenage boys what their closest friendships meant to them and documenting what they had to say.

This particular question turns out to be an issue of life or death for American men.

Before Way, no one would have thought to ask boys what was

happening in their closest friendships because we assumed we already knew. In fact, when it comes to what is happening emotionally with boys or men, we confuse what we expect of them with what they actually feel. And given enough time, they do so as well.

This surprisingly simple line of inquiry, once engaged, can open a Pandora's box of self-reflection for men. After a lifetime of being told how men "typically" experience feeling and emotion, the answer to the question "What do my closest friends mean to me?" is lost to us.

And here is the proof. In a survey published by AARP in 2010, we learn that one in three adults aged 45 or older reported being chronically lonely. Just a decade before, only one out of five of us said that. And men are facing the brunt of this epidemic of loneliness. Research shows that between 1999 and 2010 suicide among men, age 50 and over, rose by nearly 50 percent. *The New York Times* reports that "the suicide rate for middle-aged men was 27.3 deaths per 100,000, while for women it was 8.1 deaths per 100,000."

In an article for *The New Republic* titled "The Lethality of Loneliness," Judith Shulevitz writes:

Emotional isolation is ranked as high a risk factor for mortality as smoking. A partial list of the physical diseases thought to be caused by or exacerbated by loneliness would include Alzheimer's, obesity, diabetes, high blood pressure, heart disease, neurodegenerative diseases, and even cancer. Tumors can metastasize faster in lonely people.

Meanwhile, as I sat down to write about Niobe Way's research today, a tweet by Alain de Botton popped up in my stream: "An epidemic of loneliness generated by the misguided idea that romantic love is the only solution to loneliness."

And there you have it. What Niobe Way illuminates in her book is nothing less than the central source of our culture's epidemic of male loneliness.

Driven by our collective assumption that the friendships of boys are both casual and interchangeable, along with our relentless privileging of romantic love over platonic love, we are driving boys into lives Professor Way describes as "autonomous, emotionally stoic, and isolated." What's more, the traumatic loss of connection for boys Way describes is directly linked to our struggles as men in every aspect of our lives.

Way's research shows us that as boys in early adolescence, we express deeply fulfilling emotional connection and love for each other, but by the time we reach adulthood, that sense of connection evaporates.

This is a catastrophic loss; a loss we somehow assume men will simply adjust to. They do not. Millions of men are experiencing a sense of deep loss that haunts them even though they are engaged in fully realized romantic relationships, marriages and families.

For men, the voices in Way's book open a deeply private door to our pasts. In the words of the boys themselves, we experience the heartfelt expression of male emotional intimacy that echoes the sunlit afternoons of our youth. This passionate and loving boy-to-boy connection occurs across class, race and cultures. It is exclusive to neither white nor black, rich nor poor. It is universal; beautifully evident in the hundreds of interviews that Way conducted. These boys declare freely the love they feel for their closest friends. They use the word love and they are proud to do so.

Consider this quote from a 15-year-old boy named Justin:
[My best friend and I] love each other ... that's it, you have this thing that is deep, so deep, it's within you, you can't explain it. It's just a thing that you know that that person is that person and that is all that should be important in our friendship. I guess in life, sometimes two people can really, really understand each other and really have a trust, respect, and love for each other. It just happens, it's human nature.

Way writes:

Set against a culture that perceives boys and men to be activity oriented, emotionally illiterate, and interested only in independence, these stories seem shocking. The lone cowboy, the cultural icon of masculinity in the West, suggests that what boys want and need most are opportunities for competition and autonomy. Yet over 85% of the hundreds of boys we have interviewed throughout adolescence for the past 20 years suggest that their closest friendships- especially those during early and middle adolescence – share the plot of *Love Story* more than the plot of *Lord of the Flies*. Boys from different walks of life greatly valued their male friendships and saw them as critical components to their emotional wellbeing, not because their friends were worthy opponents in the competition for manhood, but because they were able to share their thoughts and feelings – their deepest secrets – with these friends.

Yet something happens to boys as they enter late adolescence. As boys enter manhood, they do, in fact, begin to talk less. They start using the phrase "no homo" following any intimate statement about their friends and they begin to say that they don't have time for their male friendships even though they continue to express strong desires for having such friendships.

In response to a simple question regarding how their friendships have changed since they were a freshman in high school, two boys respond and reveal everything about friendships for boys during adolescence. Justin describes in his senior year how his friendships have changed since he was a freshman:

I don't know, maybe, not a lot, but I guess that best friends become close friends. So that's basically the only thing that changed. It's like best friends become close friends, close friends become general friends and then general friends become acquaintances. So they just, if there's distance whether it's, I don't know, natural or whatever. You can say that, but it just happens that way.

Michael says:
Like my friendship with my best friend is fading, but I'm saying it's still there but ... so I mean, it's still there cause we still do stuff together, but only once in a while. It's sad, cause he lives only one block away from me and I get to do stuff with him less than I get to do stuff with people who are way further. It's like a DJ used his cross fader and started fading it slowly and slowly and now I'm like halfway through the cross fade.

And then Way takes us through the logical results of this disconnection for boys:

Boys know by late adolescence that their close male friendships, and even their emotional acuity, put them at risk of being labeled girly, immature, or gay. Thus, rather than focusing on who they are, they become obsessed with who they are not, they are not girls, little boys nor, in the case of heterosexual boys, are they gay. In response to a cultural context that links intimacy in male friendships with an age, a sex (female), and a sexuality (gay), these boys mature into men who are autonomous, emotionally stoic, and isolated.

The ages of 16 to 19, however, are not only a period of disconnection for the boys in my studies, it is also a period in which the suicide rate for boys in the United States rises dramatically and becomes five times the rate of girls when in early adolescence it is only three times the rate of girls. And it is the developmental period in which many of the school shootings we have read about in the paper have occurred and violence, more generally, among boys occurs. Just as boys during early and middle adolescence predicted, not having friends to share their deepest secrets appears to make them go "wacko."

In America, men perform masculinity within a narrow set of cultural rules often called the Man Box. One of the central tenets of the Man Box is the subjugation of women and by extension, all things feminine. Since we Americans hold emotional connection as a female trait, we reject it in our boys, demanding that they "man up" and adopt a strict regimen of emotional independence, even isolation as proof they are real men. Behind the drumbeat message that real men are stoic and detached, is the brutal fist of homophobia, ready to crush any boy who might show too much of the wrong kind of emotions.

And so, by late adolescence, boys declare over and over "no homo" following any intimate statement about their friends.

And so, there it is, the smoking gun, the toxic poison that is leading to the life-killing epidemic of loneliness for men, (and by extension, women,) look no further. It's right there: "no homo."

Which is why we have fought relentlessly for gay rights and marriage equality. It is a battle for the hearts and souls of our young sons. The sooner being gay is normalized, the sooner we will all be free of the shrill and violent homophobic policing of boys and men. America's pervasive homophobic, anti-feminine policing has forced generations of young men to abandon each other's support at the crucial moment they enter manhood.

It is a heart-rending realization that even as men hunger for real connection in our male relationships, we have been trained away from embracing it.

We have been trained to choose surface level relationships, even isolation; sleepwalking through our lives out of fear that we will not be viewed as real men. We keep the loving natures that once came so naturally to us hidden and locked away. This training runs so deep we're no longer even conscious of it. And we pass this training on, men and women alike, to generation after generation of bright-eyed, loving little boys.

By the time Professor Way was completing her presentation, I realized I was feeling sick. A queasy nausea roiled up. Something was uncoiling in me; something cold and bleak that had taken root in me long ago and gone to sleep there. As Way read these boys' words, it woke up. It was a baleful moment of mutual recognition. A sense of utter despair came rushing up, vast, deeper than deep. A February moment to end all of them. Spring was never coming back.

And no matter how determined I had been all those years ago to put my grief away, it was here now, a wall of pain so pure and unflinchingly raw, I was shocked to discover that something so huge could fit in the frail confines of a human being.

And even now, as I write these words, gingerly reaching out to give witness to that part of me, I am confronted with a dizzying abyss of sadness that stops my breath, leaving me flinching, waiting for the same killing blow to fall again. Over and over and over again.

I never made it to my birthday dinner. Instead, I wept for George, my wife holding me as we barreled home through the winter darkness on the New York City subway.

When I was seven, my best friend's name was George. He lived around the corner from me. George was tall and lanky. His elbows always akimbo, his cowlick stellar in its sheer verticality. He had an aquarium. He had a glow-in-the-dark board game. He had the 45 RPM of "Hang on Sloopy" and he was a Harry Nilsson fan, just like me.

I can still recall his house, the luminous joy it held for me, along with each sidewalk crack, garden and tree root that marked, step by childhood step, the block of houses separating us. I still see it in my mind's eye that way. The way in which a child sees down close to the ground, the twigs and ants and trimmed grass sprawling into distinct green blades. All part of the frozen 7-year-old's mosaic that exploded into pieces when my parents' marriage failed, launching them into the bitter self-immolation that typifies American divorce.

Boxes were packed. Doors closed and locked. We were swept away in a wave of surging dislocation, to another house, other hands, other curbs and sidewalks in another part of town. It was never to be the same. And try as I may, I cannot shake the magic of that one lost suburban street.

Although we lived just an hour apart, our parents were not willing to ensure that George and I stayed in regular contact. For my mother's part, perhaps it was just too much. Alongside a wrenching divorce, a new husband and the challenges of putting the past behind her, perhaps George was just that. Too much a thing of the past.

But George and I were granted a yearly reprieve. Once or sometimes twice a year, George and I were allowed a sleepover. George always came to spend the night on my birthday. It was the one gift I asked for. His visit.

We would spend all night sorting and reading mountains of comics books. Drawing superheroes and discussing, page by page, the comic art of Neal Adams, Jack Kirby, Jim Aparo, Bernie Wrightson, Frank Frazetta and all the others. We loved that artwork. Each line and pen stroke. Each page. I recall we were also able to meet at a few comic conventions. Watching Harryhausen films and searching thousands of musty boxes for back issues.

Then one day it ended. My mother simply said, "No more." I still feel it in my gut. Like a knife so sharp that all I felt was the intense cold of it.

Did I ask why? One time? A hundred times? I don't recall. My mother was never one for questions about her decisions.

To this day, I don't know what triggered that choice for her, but my guess is she was feeling vaguely uncomfortable. That two boys, by then around eleven years old, should be moving on to things more productive than comic books and sleepovers. That this "friendship" should have died of its own lack of oxygen, but, pending that, she could no longer sponsor something so ... intense. From her perspective, it was unnaturally so.

How many times have we heard parents say, "Oh, they'll make new friends." As if the relationships of children are so shallow and contextual that they can be swapped out like last year's lunchbox. Whatever kid they are seated by, in whatever random schoolroom is assigned, will do as well as the next.

George and I dutifully gave up our friendship, like boys are trained to do, when some random life change demands it of us. I accepted the arcane logic of my mother's decision and turned away to other relationships more convenient to her purposes.

I'm sorry to hold her responsible in this way. I would like to leave, somehow, petals of kind recollections trailing along the internet, holding her memory aloft, but I don't have it in me. Her choices were too dysfunctional, too emotionally exhausted, too tired, dismissive, numbing, too predictable.

When I was in my early thirties, I ran into George again. He was working for a local newspaper and living in an apartment in Houston. I went and visited him. To my surprise, he happily split up his comic collection and gave me half of his huge collection. (I had sold mine when I was 16 or so.) It was an act of profound generosity and I'm sure I was effusive in my thanks.

Then I ran into George again in my forties. He had married, moved to California and was living south of L.A. near Seal Beach. On a business trip, I spent the night at his house. We fell into our old pattern of reading comic books and drawing while his wife hovered, declaring over and over how great it was that I was visiting. The next day I packed up and went home to New York feeling vaguely disconnected, but happy.

A year and a half later, I boxed up a bunch of new graphic novels and mailed them to George with a note telling him that these were my new favorites. To this day, I'm not sure what instinct caused me to make that final gesture.

About six months later his wife called me. She was screaming and weeping, this woman I had only met for a few short hours. George had died.

To this day, I remain shocked. Why didn't I connect more, was my first thought. My second was how effusive his wife had been about my visit. So supportive. So happy for "George's friend" to be there. I was never able to follow up after his death. I don't even know what killed him, just an illness. Strangely, when I collected my thoughts, I realized I could no longer find a phone number for George's wife. She had called me on a land line? I don't remember. Maybe I did call her one more time. A fog of disconnection rises in me about this. Just move on. Just move on.

I recall a single phone call with his mother after his death. (Had she called me?) If I go into my decades-old contact list today, I have no entry for George. No address in L.A. No disconnected email address. Nothing.

How is this possible? How did I sleepwalk through the chance to reconnect with this friendship? I should have cared. I should have given a damn. Why didn't I? Because somewhere, somehow, I was convinced that close friendships with boys are too painful?

Don't parents understand? Don't they know that we love each other? That our children's hearts can be broken so profoundly that we will never rise to a love like that again?

What boys do, the world had convinced me, was to move on to the next thing. So, I did so. We shrug our collective shoulders and suppress the panic of heartbreak and loss. We go numb. We suppress everything. We accept the world as a surface-level exercise. Because the love boys feel, that passion we feel for the ones we love is too powerful. It makes grownups nervous.

And we can't have grownups feeling nervous now, can we?

Let's take a moment to connect the dots:

1. Boys feel fierce love for their best friends
2. Add homophobia, the Man Box, etc.

3. Boys disassociate from loving best friends
4. Boys and men become emotionally isolated
5. Men enter the epidemic of loneliness
6. Men die

We now have a clear and direct through-line tying rampant homophobia and the Man Box to resulting grief, isolation, and early mortality in heterosexual men.

Sound a little dramatic? Here is the central piece of research data that every man should take to heart.

In a 6-year study of 736 middle-aged men, attachment to a single person (almost always a spouse) did NOT lower the risk of heart attack and fatal coronary heart disease, whereas having a strong social support network did. (Kristina Orth-Gomer, Annika Rosengren & Lars Wilhelmsen, "Lack of Social Support and Incidence of Coronary Heart Disease in Middle-Aged Swedish Men," *Psychosomatic Medicine*, 55 (1993): 37–43)

I recall to this day, walking into George's room when I was ten and him holding out a copy of Jack Kirby's *New Gods*. The issue was titled "The Death Wish of Terrible Turpin." His joy in sharing that with me, the book thrust out in his hands, is as real to me now as any human moment I can recall. The birth of my son. My dear wife's tears. Anything.

When I turn my thoughts to those times with George, I feel a glimmer of primal emotional power glowing in me. Something fierce and unquenched is there. Something I badly need to reconnect to.

Niobe Way has given us a clear and actionable truth about boys and about ourselves as men. We can shrug it off at our peril. But ignoring her truth and the truth of these boys comes with a terrible price.

The loss of my friendship with George set a pattern in my life that I am only now, decades later, finally conscious of. I have walked past so many friendships. Sleepwalking past men, as I went instead from woman to woman, looking for everything I had lost. Looking instead in the realm of the romantic, the sexual. A false lead to a false solution. And in doing so, I have missed so many opportunities to live a fuller life.

Our female or male lovers are not put here to replace the warm, platonic love of the hilarious, generous, sympathetic men in our lives. They are put here to celebrate them with us, even as we celebrate our lover's passionate platonic friends with them. It is a symphony of love, wherein our joy in platonic love is co-amplified by our sexual loves. Both.

Since my birthday I have placed some phone calls. I called my friend Michael and I told him I love him. That I value him as one of my closest friends and that I welcome him to call on me for fun or for sorrow. I have told my story several times to other friends, like I'm telling it here, and in doing so, I'm becoming fierce and awake now.

Niobe Way's work has given me the piece of the puzzle I was never conscious of. That the love I had felt for George and others, Troy, Jack, David, Bruce, and Kyle, was right and good and powerful. Could move mountains. I didn't realize what they were then. But I do now. That the slow withdrawing of those friendships from my life had not been a killing blow. Not quite. And that I'm back in the game of loving my friends. Fiercely.

So, know it guys. I love you all.

When Men Make "I'm Sorry" Into a Weapon

We all have our personal histories. I have mine.
Decades ago, my story became monolithic. It ceased to be a collection of distinct events, instead becoming a larger singular narrative.

The story feels very big and very old, a heavy stone, sitting in my gut. It raises hackles when I examine it. When I approach it, it shifts into something angry and raging; something locked away at the bottom of the basement stairs, threatening me with every step I take towards it.

In first noting its presence decades ago, I saw and understood its damaging influence. This is an important first step in learning who we are. To put a crucial little bit of space between what we feel in the moment and the much longer history of our lives that informs and drives those feelings. We come to understand that our response to this world is not just a response to what takes place around us, it is filtered through the history of relationships and events that make up our story.

I have tried to go down into the darkness and deal with this thing, this stone. I have warily circled it. At times, I have laid siege to it with too few troops and too little commitment, eventually backing away, satisfied that I put it on notice. An act of self-reflection and of courage, yes, but also a plateau.

What made this angry thing? Who put this here? My absent father? My overwhelmed mother? A 50-year-old divorce? Violence? Being a victim? Being invisible? Is this thing still growing and changing right now, or did what made it finish its work long, long ago?

The history of my life, my actions over decades, I catalogue and assign good and bad values. I shame myself or I give myself a bit of credit. "I did all right by that person." But this thing in my gut is always there. Jump scare lurching up, creating this low buzz of anxiety like the throb of engines underground.

I have written about manhood for almost ten years. The more I deconstruct our cultural narratives of what a "real man" is, the more my sense of agency grows. I'm seeing the patterns of how I got here, the reasons for every act of policing and violence that made me wary and uncertain about what other boys and men might do to me even to this day, are still doing to me, over and over in my stories.

After ten years of examining what our abusive culture of manhood does to boys and men, and how that intersects with my own stories, the question arrives, like an old man walking up a road. Slowly.

"What is your shame? Even to this day?"

I go looking further into my abiding sense of being cheated, and bingo, there it is. Stop right there. Being cheated.

And a chip flakes off of the stone in my gut.

Being cheated. Hold that one idea.

I was clearly cheated. Yes, I was. You're goddamn right I was. I was cheated out of a chance to be a complete young man as I went through the process of growing up; to become the bright, confident, caring person I could have become. Instead, for a long time, I was stunted, broken and angry.

Dozens of beautiful, potentially life-long relationships and friendships came and went. People drifted past, disconnected. Isolation was there, regardless of who loved me or where I was. Loneliness, an old record skipping, skipping.

This is a good life but I still feel anxious.

This is a good marriage but I'm somehow missing it.

So, I work and work to prove I'm a caring person and a good partner, like I'm paying off a debt I can never pay off. Like I'm making up for something lacking. Like I'm not enough.

I was cheated. Yes, I was. I was cheated out of being a whole person and there's nothing I can do about it.

I'm on a treadwheel, making up for something. Erasing my failures, my shame, but it never ends; the debt accrues, growing.

And the thing in my gut shifts a bit. Massive, immutable. Impossible to name.

The plateau I reached all those years ago? Laying siege to the thing in my gut but never fully confronting it? Lord knows I tried, right? I have been careful to always apologize for its being there; always apologizing.

Men say it all the time. I'm sorry for being messed up like this. So, let me fix something. Can I fix something for you? Or you? Or you?

And we say I'm sorry for these things I'm feeling.

I'm sorry.

What did I just say? Do I say that a lot?

When we do the work to become better men. When we do the work as it is called, we confront our stories and delve into our shadows. In these moments, we are not simply seeking to put the past to rest. That is part of it, but the past is never the past. The past is right now, and the past is active, in motion, moving through our lives. The past has agency and power.

As men, we know the past is here with us, even as we lash out, or implode, self-denigrate or struggle to get out of bed in the morning. And so, we apologize for our failings over and over and over again, because we're good men, right? Just a bit broken. Just a bit wounded. We were victims and it's so hard, you see ... What do you want me to say? I'm sorry about the way things are. All right? I said I'm sorry.

There it is. The club in my hand. "I'm sorry."

Watch me hit myself with the club. "I'm sorry."

And so comes the moment in which it fully dawns on me. I'm not the victim anymore. I'm something else.

"I'm sorry." WHAM. See the blood spray off?

It's a heavy powerful club. It's dented and hard.

"Oh, you didn't see that blow? You didn't see my blood? Maybe you glanced away? Let me do it again for you."

"I'm sorry."

And suddenly, I'm seeing it in my hand. This club. It is a shock to truly and finally see it.

I know for some of you, this violent metaphor might be alarming, but let me ask us to step back now and I'll try and make sense of it.

First and foremost, the club is not real. There is no blood. But this metaphor of a club represents a thing that I have found myself doing that is central to what holds me back in my own life. I suspect many men might face a similar challenge.

For so very many of us, "I'm sorry" is not an apology. It's a threat.

At some point in my teens, my self-loathing settled over everything. I chose self-loathing as my story not because I had any control over what had happened to me as a young boy, but because it was the only way I felt a sense of connection to others; to confess my disgust with myself to them. Over and over and over.

Throughout my teens and early twenties, I performed my shame. It had an impact. Maybe it got someone to back off, maybe it got me a momentary expression of pity, maybe a night in someone's bed, maybe it got me a shocked expression. It got me something. Looking back, I suspect that it was the only significant part of me I could reliably conjure up. It became my crutch; this performance of my authentic shame that I publicly displayed over and over.

But we human beings are remarkably resilient animals. We

grow and change and we learn to cope. And so, as the years passed, my public shame went underground. Like many men, I grew my sense of agency by learning to earn money, buy a house, form relationships. These are our cultural symbols of confidence and validation.

Additionally, I learned to acknowledge a more complete view of myself, reducing the influence of my shame and grief, perhaps driving it into the basement, no? Ultimately, I started asking hard questions about being a father and a man in America, getting at the reasons why one boy's childhood could have been so systemically caustic.

In the years since, my power to design and create has grown into a substantial part of me, the result of my work to change and become a person who could love and be loved. Eventually some peace arrived, but it overlaid a continuing current of agitation, of anxiety; a deep black river, flowing underground.

And so, when I sometimes falter and fail, I say, "I'm sorry." As if my failings are not simply human, but instead, proof of a larger narrative of defeat for me. A continuation of an old, old story. Proof I haven't made it yet. And maybe, never will? What a strangely familiar and comforting idea that is ...

And then I know my victim-self is in the room, in the way I can still feel the familiar in the frantic. In the way I work so very hard to display what I am learning or creating. In the way I write these articles. I am the guy in the room whose voice pitches up, my excitement makes my words tumble out. Excitement and anxiety, blending. But I'm a good guy, right? I'm doing pretty well. I'm just anxious because I had a rough time of it.

And, sometimes, when things get raw or real or challenging ... "I'm sorry."

And then, the stone truly shifts.

It might be spoken softly, or cheerfully. It may be because I forget something from the store, or because I didn't let someone finish telling me why they are feeling hurt by me. Something little or something big, and if I'm feeling stretched a bit thin today, not every day, but perhaps today, out pops, "I'm sorry for what I did."

And there it is, the warning.

But the conversation doesn't stop. It goes a bit further and the basement door swings open. Something comes lurching up the stairs from the darkness. Then the room is spinning a little and my body is getting hot and ... "I'm sorry for who I am."

Not so gentle this time. Not so easily dismissed.

Wham! Into the room it lurches.

Do what I want or I will display my shame. It will show up as anger or a display of grief or disgust with myself. I will take a hostage (me), and I will abuse that hostage until you back off or give me what I want.

Not a confidence builder. Not the actions of a good man.

So, here's the thing about doing the work. You seek to deal with your past and your moods and your shame and it can feel ugly and powerless and sickening. The work is difficult and it's never ending, and you push, and trudge, and seek, and struggle, and you start to feel like you maybe have a handle on a few more things, and then you look down and there's a bloody club in your hand. And you say, "uh, oh."

And then, to make it even more complicated, others in your life say things like, "Nice article, only I don't see you that way. Not at all."

Big breath.

Which leaves me wondering why I'm still constructing this idea of myself as a victimized person, full of self-loathing. Why am I giving free rent to that idea?

It has to do with the crutch victimhood and shame supplies us, men and women alike. As long as I'm broken, I can be exhausted. As long as I'm struggling, I can fail. As long as I'm still in that fight, I can go on being wounded and every little success I have is a miracle instead of just the normal daily moments of living with integrity.

We need the story of being broken, so we can keep others at bay, so we can take a pass on being held accountable.

When you study and write about men you run headlong into ideas like friend zone, nice guys, cucks, white knights, gold diggers, and a hundred other destructive, misogynist narratives that ALWAYS come back to this idea for men of being cheated; of fighting back from a place of self-assigned and fiercely held victimhood. And as easy as it is to see that pattern in those men who are openly blaming women and raging at the world, the roots of victimhood run deep in many of us, men and women alike.

So, I tell my story in an effort to invite men like me to self-reflect on the more subtle ways we seek to leverage our victimhood. When we "good men" take up that club of self-loathing and threaten to beat ourselves bloody in order to back others off, avoid our own accountability or coerce others to do what we want, we are coming from a place of damage and creating more of it.

Some would have us believe we men intentionally use our victimhood in this way. That we cynically trot out our self-loathing in an effort to force our wives, husbands, friends or children to shift from self-assertion to care giving. Or flay ourselves in the public square as a way to sidestep our responsibility to make a better world, performing a gaudy caricature of suffering and rage that avoids the hard work of being in community.

I don't hold this manipulative leveraging of victimhood to be the norm. It is my opinion that many men truly feel they are poisonous, damaged, alone. The challenge is not whether our victimhood is authentic. God knows the world has millions of ways to shame and degrade men and women alike.

The challenge is how long will we remain stuck on the plateau? This vast space in which we remain in a decades-old standoff with our past demons instead of doing the work to reintegrate them into our hearts and lives? Yes, the first part of the work is to see and name our demons, but that is only half of the work. Many of us are at risk of remaining on that lonely plateau, where we host our demons, fearing to let go of the dark power they grant us.

"I'm sorry."

No, actually, you are not.

So, let me share this: I have leveraged my victimhood to avoid my responsibilities to the people I love. I have used it as a crutch and a tool and a weapon to force compliance, so much so, that some of the people I once loved have simply walked away.

As long as I continue to perform powerlessness in relation to my past, I am stealing joy from those I love. If I do not discard the club in my hand, I am failing to reach my potential in the world and others will suffer for it. For me, remaining on the plateau is a selfish choice. It is a place where I hold myself accountable for nothing and do my work for no one. It is a plateau of intentional self-isolation. Whatever benefit choosing to center my victimhood provided in my young life, that benefit is long finished. It's time to let it go, brothers.

And so, as a father and a husband and a human being, I have a responsibility to drop this club I am carrying and walk on without it. Instead of using it when things get tough, I will have to face my demons that lurch up, raging, and own the fact that I have kept them intentionally as leverage against the world.

I have a responsibility to start treating people fairly – myself, most of all. I can make the simple choice not to feed off my shame anymore. It wasn't my fault. I was too small to stop it. I didn't cause it. And it was long ago.

For those I love, I commit to no more hostage taking, no more threats, no more abusive behaviour cloaked in shame. For those who love me, I'm deeply grateful for your patience as I took the time to figure this piece out. You are amazing people.

And myself? What am I? I am a man with lots more work to do. I am also a loving man of integrity.

Then I See Him Laughing

Think of this as a poem.

Like most parents, I live in the dual spaces of ecstatic joy and plodding effortfullness. Working at getting things done that a parent needs to get done, as if that is somehow the purpose of living ... getting things done. The decades-long process of raising a child puts one at constant risk for the loss of spontaneity and play. Replaced with talking at and lists. Do this. Do that. Get it done. And for whom? Whose lists are these anyway?

We become calliopes of demand, honking and clanging at our children, fueled by consumerism, and success panic, leading ultimately to what? Taskmaster as love? Doing as being? *Leaving,* most likely. The empty nest. The goodbye.

I saw it in my exhausted departure from my own mother's house. We finally released our mutual chokehold when I turned eighteen and I walked out to a friend's car to disappear from her orderly life. Not remotely prepared for the world but going anyway. She has not really seen me since. A few moments of connection, honest moments I can count on one hand.

There is the pang of missed opportunities that remains across all the years, a generations-old emotional stone that spreads its chilly ripples as I struggle to be a lively, engaged parent to my son. What's the use? It's going to go to shit. Arguments about car keys and back talk. The shattering of increasingly brittle trust and paths that lead to darkened emotional spaces, dirty and disorganized. Leave the lights off. It's better not looking.

And then I see him laughing, and I'm laughing too. We're across from each other on a chilly morning in December, just days ago, our knees touching. A warm cup in my hand. The floor cluttered with cast-off items and wadded paper. The table piled with drawings and plates, logjams of colored pencils. The explosive laughter grows as we realize the second, the third layer of the joke, seeing that realization blooming in each other's eyes. Oh man, RIGHT NOW we're never gone. So hard to remember. So hard to declare.

We can be grief-stricken animals if we let fear be our lead story. Loss becomes our only valid signpost for living. Loss is our marker that something real has happened. And so, our future is irrevocably defined by the events of our past when we had no choice, no control.

Well, to hell with that.

Because inside me, when I fall into that funerary mindset, that rainy, droning burial of my child's hopes, my anger rises to meet it. My son has the courage to laugh. My son has a light in his eyes that startles me with its intensity, humor, mischievous joy and strength of will. My son sings, "Get up, stand up" and dances across the living room.

And in a flash, I follow my anger up and out. What the hell? For my sweet laughing wife. For my son, bright eyed and beautifully chaos smitten. For every child standing in the shadow of judgment and policing, I follow it up. My anger is my shield and my sword against the stupid, repeating, idiotic stories of failure we cut our milk teeth on. Enough of that. Enough.

So, forget the eventual departures, the bleak conjuring of crushed bicycles and police tape or the cold loss of alienation. All the dark fears we conjure for ourselves. Whatever is coming is coming. Shake your fist at what's coming and turn your attention to now. Right now.

Hold your child close and tell him/her loud and clear. "I love you so much, *I can't stand it!*"

They'll know exactly what you mean.

Afterword

In closing, let me *thank you* for your interest in *Remaking Manhood*. I am truly grateful.

Remaking Manhood represents my contribution over a period of years to the life-changing conversation about men that is emerging all around us.

If you're willing to help share my work, here's what you can do:

1. "Like" our Remaking Manhood page on Facebook and share links to some of our articles or videos.
   https://www.facebook.com/remakingmanhood
   A positive comment to your community about our book and our work to grow children's relational intelligence will work wonders.
2. Also, please consider visiting **RemakingManhood.com** and signing up for our mailing list.
3. Finally, write a short review and rate *Remaking Manhood* on our book's page on Amazon.com.

Thanks so much! Your help will make all the difference.

Warm regards,

Mark Greene
@RemakingManhood
Facebook.com/RemakingManhood
RemakingManhood.com

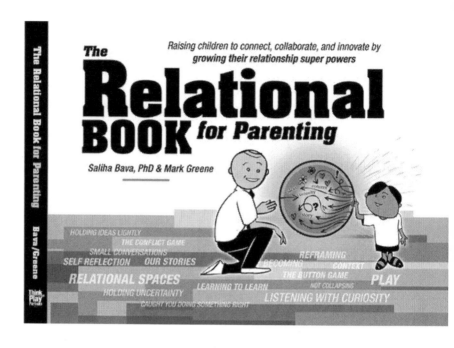

New from Mark Greene and Saliha Bava:
The Relational Book for Parenting

    The ability to create healthy, authentic relationships will be the key to our children's personal and professional success over the course of their lifetimes. Co-authors Saliha Bava, PhD and Mark Greene's book is a playful mix of comics, fables, games and powerful hands-on relational ideas. It's a playful path to ensure our children's ability to connect, collaborate, and innovate by growing their relationship superpowers.

Learn more at ThinkPlayPartners.com

55938578R00087

Made in the USA
Columbia, SC
20 April 2019